THE ROCK STAR RETIREMENT PROGRAMME

DOMINIC WATSON

For legal reasons I am obliged to state the following:

Within the fullest extent permitted by law, I am providing this written material and all associated resources on an 'as is' basis and make no (and expressly disclaim all) representations and warranties of any kind in the respect to this written material or its contents including, without limitation, advice and recommendations, warranties or merchantability and fitness for a particular purpose. The author will not be liable for any damages arising out of or in connection with the use of this written material. This is a comprehensive limitation of liability that applied to all damages of any kind including (without limitation) compensatory, direct, indirect or consequential damages, loss of data, income or profit, loss or damage to any property and claims of third parties.

What the above says is I'm simply showing you what might be achieved not telling you what to do!

FOR MY FAMILY

ACKNOWLEDGEMENTS

With thanks to:

My wife Julie for holding the fort and buying me the time to write a book on top of what was and is an already incredibly busy life.

Julia Ibbotson for insightful tips during my first year of writing and to my good friend Tamsin Caine for offering your mum's support!

The team at Northwich Library whose signs encouraged me to start thinking about writing a book in the first place;

Robert J Holmes for inspiring the book concept and remaining dignified and retaining a wicked sense of humour when life threw the kitchen sink at you;

Alan and Vicki Wilcox for being my first ever sounding board for the concept of this book and for giving me the confidence to run with it;

Julie Williams for showing an interest and then taking the time to read the first embryonic draft and helping me to begin to shape it and take it to the next level;

My editor and long-suffering writing mentor, Taryn Johnston who had to manage the explosion of ideas that this book became and had the difficult task of killing my numerous darlings. And for providing the cakes.

The late Roy 'Razzer' Clarke and to all at Razzers Runners for giving me my love of running and a second lease of life and to Northwich Running Club for keeping running interesting;

Michael Roberts for putting up with my constant diatribe about this project and for being my first ever proper running friend;

John Bandachino and Liz Calcutt for being reliable sources of common sense and honesty throughout the three years of this project;

My creators and nurturers — my mum and dad (yep dad, I did manage to finish the book before you departed this mortal coil, now please hang around for the follow up);

My sister whose musical endeavours will continue to amuse me for the rest of my life;

My mentors and wise old sages, Patrick Myers and Tony Tindale and my virtual mentors, Brian Tracy and Isiah Hankel.

David Hyner for inspiring me to set "big fat hairy goals" and for invaluable practical follow up advice on how to achieve them.

The staff at Viva Coffee and Juice Bar Northwich for their inspirational wall quote and hospitality;

The Canal and River Trust for helping to hook me up with some great 'case studies;'

Brice and Sheila Napier for giving me an insight into their world and encouraging me to spread the news;

John White and Robina Moss for publishing my first articles and giving me the confidence to write more and for Robina's later input in tidying up the final manuscript.

To Claire Pattison and Neil Simpson, the team at the School of Business and Law at Manchester Metropolitan University for helping me to improve my time management skills and task prioritisation which ultimately enabled me to get the book finished and over the line.

TESTIMONIALS

"I was so immersed in your book I actually lost track of time! Powerful and alighting stuff. It gave me a whole new perspective of life. I feel really privileged to be one of the first people to read it."

— CODILIA GAPARE, award-winning entrepreneur.

"All my life I have done something I have loved, whether racing or raising money for charity, so for me there has never been any thought of retiring and I think that's what Dom captures here in this book. Living life to the full is the best way to "retire". This book is a must whether you're 28 or 98"

— BOB CHAMPION MBE

"Even though I am still in my 30s, an incredibly relevant, motivational and practical read that I would recommend to anybody seeking to improve their lot in life"

— ADE OJOSIPI, business owner

"Congratulations Dominic! This is a beautiful book. I hope you sell a million!"

— BRIAN TRACY

5.0 out of 5 stars new concepts in retirement planning
15 January 2019

I am planning my retirement and have been reading about it and attending various professional forums as well.

Invariably discussion is around financial arrangements and retirement age etc.

I became aware of a strange study about consultant doctors in NHS. Majority of them were healthy individuals but succumb to death or chronic illnesses with in 2-3 years after their retirement. There were no financial or other stresses in their retired life.

Later on it appeared that sudden departure from an active and busy life style lead to mental issues and consequent ill health problems. Now there is an active drive for senior health professionals to plan their retirement at least 2-3 years before retirement and preferably phase in the retirement to adjust to retired life.

There is active encouragement to have postretirement lifestyle adjustment to avoid mental health shocks.

I was pleasantly surprised to see Dominic's book which has addressed this issue. He has gone a step forward to break the myth of fixed retirement age. New definition seems to be retire at any age to do what one enjoys in life rather than how much to earn in retirement. This is a paradigm shift in concept of retirement. This was taken for granted to retire at 65 years of age and then wait for death.

Dominic has introduced the concept of retirement to enjoy your life ambitions and age is not the bar to wait for.

He has very professionally introduced physiology of human body and psychology of human mind for lay persons and how it responds to life events both positive and negative.

I was very impressed by the techniques he has suggested to make rational decisions and cope with them.

Real life stories of people at different stages of life are very inspiring and road map for potential retirees.

There is a comprehensive chapter on different financial models to fund the retirement. I will recommend to read this again and again as it is an eye-opener for naïve s like me with head in the sand.

I will recommend this book to everyone to read at every stage of life and make informed decisions rather than remain aloof.

Accompanying web site has got wealth of information and is highly recommended.

—MR SM CHAUDHARY, consultant eye surgeon

"Above all this is a 'how to' book that is enthralling, will make you smile, look forward to fun and fulfilment and give you the map and tools to 'retire' on your terms as early as you possibly can. To use a cliché I've never used before in any of my reviews this book 'should be prescribed free by the NHS' as it delivers happiness, healthy minds and bodies. Fulfilled individuals leaving as their legacy 'a mark not a scar' means a more compassionate society too. The 'Rockstar Retirement Programme' #rocks"

— TONY ROBINSON

THE SETLIST

Introduction   **11**

About The Author   **17**

What Is Retirement?   **18**

What Is Wrong With The Current Advice?   **23**

Lesson 1 — Settle Your Scores And Seize The Day   **35**

Lesson 2 — 50 Shades Of Grey   **53**

Lesson 3 — Rock Star Health   **81**

Lesson 4 — Drugs And Rock And Roll   **95**

Lesson 5 — Rock Star Ageing   **103**

Lesson 6 — Rock Star Focus   **119**

Lesson 7 — Rock Star Priorities   **141**

Lesson 8 — What Should *Your* Rock Star Retirement Look Like?   **157**

Lesson 9 — Funding Your Rock Star Retirement   **185**

Lesson 10 — Creating A Rock Star Legacy   **241**

The Power Of Belief   **242**

Conclusion   **279**

Frank went into IT relatively late in his career and his job title of 'Software Support Consultant' used to give him great pride. Unfortunately though, as the company grew, his role became little more than working in a glorified call centre. He is now 58 and almost three times the age of some of his work colleagues. When he is at work he feels like an outsider. In fact, he no longer knows where he belongs. **However, Frank used to have a dream about his retirement. He was going to own a bar in Tenerife, but somehow** *life just got in the way.*

Back on the other side of the world, some 13 hours ahead, Ian has finished his coffee and is checking his diary. Even though he has been *retired* for over three years, it is going to be another busy week. Next Friday he turns 48 and there is an awful lot to fit in. He has three rounds of golf, a salsa lesson, and a birthday meal with his girlfriend. On Sunday he is being picked up for an all-day trip with the walking club. There is also one other item on this week's agenda, he has a meeting with the MD of a civil engineering company who is keen to persuade him to do some consultancy work.

Extra money can sometimes be a good thing, but Ian does not need to work and he needs to find out whether the job suits him. As a civil engineer, he still enjoys the stimulation of some work projects but he can now afford to pick and choose. If he decides to work for a few weeks or even the odd month on a project, it has to be with people he likes and to be suitably interesting, without being stressful. Any work he does now needs to provide sufficient financial reward to make it worth his while sacrificing a few rounds of golf. Although, the extra money does help him to pay for better hotels and restaurants whilst he steadily ticks off places in the world he wants to visit from his 'bucket list.'

Before I go any further, it is important to point out that this is not some fictitious allegory. **Ian and Frank are real people,** as are all the other characters and case studies throughout this book. Ian used to rent a room in my first home and is one of my closest friends, although it has become a long distance friendship, as I am still based in England. I got to know Frank more recently via my working life.

It is worth highlighting that Ian and Frank had very similar starts in life and possess roughly equal IQ's. In their early years, they were also pretty outgoing and sociable. As you would expect, Ian is great fun to be around; his positivity and enthusiasm for life are infectious. Frank, however, is the opposite, he is a total energy drain. After a few minutes of interaction with him even the most chirpy, optimistic people begin to feel depressed.

So how did Ian and Frank's lives diverge so dramatically and what can we learn from this? How can you live a life on your own terms like Ian and avoid taking the path of helpless resignation that Frank has navigated to? If you recognise any of Frank's traits in yourself, or perhaps someone you know, you may also want to question whether there is any hope for Frank, or is it too late?

Ian is living life the way he wants to, one of abundance. A life in which his time and choices are his own. But to achieve this, he sought out and eventually found the knowledge to create the life he desired. Just as crucially, he applied the principals and practices he discovered on a regular and sustained basis for many years. Ian is not alone, there are many other people out there who have followed the same path, or are beginning to. Their idea of what constitutes a dream life may be very different from Ian's, but the principal of living life on your own terms, of being in control, is exactly the same; as is the recipe, the plan of action that you need to execute to get there.

Welcome to the Rock Star Retirement Plan!

Unlike Ian, you don't have to spend many years seeking out and learning the secrets of how to obtain your dream lifestyle. **You hold the keys and have the first part of the map right now; your journey began when you started to read this book**. The fundamental question is what are you going to do with the precious knowledge you are about to discover? **Do you really want a better life going forward? Do you want it enough?** Having the knowledge, the plan and the tools are all essential; however, these things alone are not enough. To change and shape your life to the way you want it to be, you need to change what you do in the present, on a regular basis. You have to follow the plan, consistently day-after-day, week-after-week. It is easy to get fired up for an initial period, but keeping the momentum going and avoiding reverting to the original status quo is not easy. The perfect illustration of how challenging this can be is provided by the weight loss industry.

Time for a diet of a different kind?

Most overweight people know the path that they must take to shed their excess pounds. The route map is pretty simple:

★ Eat less
★ Eat more healthily
★ Exercise more

Simple, yet not so easy to apply on a regular basis!

Despite thinking of ourselves as the cleverest animal, the top dog, as a species humans seem to have a disposition for **instant gratification**. We have a tendency to look for instant fixes, whether it's the short-term sugar rush from a chocolate bar 'pick me up' each day, or the crash diet to try to fix the resulting weight gain. **Neither is destined to work or afford long-term satisfaction.** What is required is a change of mind-set and a change of lifestyle over a sustained period of time.

And food is just the tip of the iceberg, we also have a tendency to binge on other things too. Most people in our modern consumer societies just keep looking for the next new thing. We seek instant satisfaction by buying things, often with money we have not yet earned, and by doing so, financial independence becomes further away as the majority of time is spent earning money to pay for the credit card or loan interest, often long after we have ceased to enjoy or even use the thing we bought to get our instant fix.

Don't worry, I will be teaching you a number of highly successful techniques and life-hacks to help you stay on track. Think of this programme as your personal trainer for getting your life into shape. Regardless of your phase of life and your current reality, we will work together to review and understand what you really want out of life. This may take you on an unexpected journey. When you reflect carefully and honestly about what you really seek, this may be quite different from what you have previously told yourself. But once we have reviewed and reframed your aspirations, we will then go on to define what your own true Rock Star Retirement looks like and map out how you can get it.

Unlike Ian though, you don't have to spend years figuring things out for yourself. I will show you that not everything in the world is quite as it seems. Having opened your eyes to your true current reality, we will then look at case studies to illustrate the full spectrum of possibilities available for an alternative and better reality. This is not a prescriptive 'how to' manual but rather a programme to help you devise and implement your own strategy, based on the experiences and examples of the many pioneers who have gone before you to lead the way.

This book is designed for:

★ Intelligent, forward-thinking people seeking to improve and shape their lives with optimism and purpose;
★ People who are considering retirement, already retired or semi-retired, aged anywhere between 39 and 99, wanting to get the most out of life!

This book is **NOT** suitable for those people who want to:

★ Scrimp and save to ensure that their children have an amazing inheritance *at their sacrifice*.
★ Line their financial adviser's pockets, or contribute towards yet more bankers' bonuses.
★ Spend their later years in the corner knitting or curled up on the couch watching daytime TV in their slippers.
★ Find a 'get rich quick' scheme, or a magical life-changing system that involves **no effort or work.**

To get the most out of this book you **DO NOT NEED**:

★ To be wealthy or rich in the conventional sense;
★ To appear younger than you are, or to be good looking like an ageing movie star (although many congratulations if you are!)

To get the most out of this book you will need:

★ An open mind;
★ A strong desire to get more from your life, both today and in the future;
★ A sense of humour. (No matter how ambitious, talented, successful or hard working you are, it is never a good idea to take yourself, or life too seriously).
★ To take action on the activities and strategies outlined to help you take control and to shape your life the way you want to live it.

So what are we waiting for? Let's get started!

ABOUT THE AUTHOR

Dominic Watson has spent the majority of his working life as a specialist business broker and management consultant, helping owners of small to medium sized businesses to sell their enterprises and to plan for retirement, or a change of lifestyle, focus or career.

He has had the unique insight of watching thousands of people plan and enter the retirement phase of their lives. He has helped many of these people to go on to live highly rewarding post working lives, or alternative career paths. He has observed and actively sought out the answers to what works and leads to happiness and what does not.

Dominic is regularly asked to provide talks by organisations such as NatWest Bank, Optix Software, Cardiff University and the Association of Independent Opticians to help people plan for their future. At the time of writing, he was in his mid-40s and lived with his wife and two young sons in an idyllic village in the beautiful Cheshire countryside. As you will discover as you read this book, Dominic was practising what he preaches and is well on track with his own Rock Star Retirement Programme, living life to the full on all levels.

Please connect with Dom on
Facebook 📘 www.facebook.com/RockstarRetirementProgramme
Twitter 🐦 @RockstarRetire

WHAT IS RETIREMENT?

If you were to ask a selection of random people for their definition of 'retirement,' you would quickly discover that it means often contrasting things to different people. It is a highly emotive subject, evoking quite polar feelings and expectations. For some people, retirement is anticipated keenly. It is perceived as some sort of utopia; a golden age. I am often amazed by people in their 30s who are already counting down the years until their retirement, with a very real danger that they will forget to enjoy their time and live fully through all the phases of their lives.

For others, the subject of retirement is dreaded and any form of planning is to be avoided. For these people, retirement signifies that their best years are behind them and that it is just a steady downward spiral in lifestyle and capability.

For some there can be a feeling of helplessness at the amount of money that needs to be saved to afford a comfortable lifestyle in their later years.

So who is right and does the level of your savings and pension pot define how happy you will be in retirement? Is there a magic number that you need in the bank to ensure success?

The great news is that, while having more money does help by providing more possibilities, I believe with a passion that with the right knowledge and approach, almost anyone can live their own version of a Rock Star Retirement lifestyle.

Retirement in its purest and most desirable form is simply **buying** time to spend doing what you really want to be doing. It is about having a choice and taking back control over your life and your time. This has a cost, but it is not necessarily a monetary pot that you have to buy from a financial services company.

This book is all about getting you to think more deeply about what retirement really means and to get you to carefully define what you want your life and retirement to look like. Once you have reframed your destination, you can make a plan and map out a path to getting there. Get it right and the journey should be equally as enjoyable as the destination.

Over the years, in my role as a consultant and business broker, I have worked with thousands of people making the transition between a busy work life and retirement. When I first started selling businesses, my focus was extremely narrow and very corporate. I concentrated on getting the best possible deals for my clients' businesses. The key measures of success I used were simply how much money I could raise for their retirement and how quickly and efficiently we could get the sale through to allow them to move onto the next phase of their lives. As I became more experienced and received real life feedback on the longer-term results, I began to notice patterns and trends. I soon discovered that although I was fulfilling my defined role by focusing on maximising the money that my clients walked away with, this did not automatically result in happiness. To my real surprise, during the early years a few of my clients even came back to me, looking to buy a replacement business to fill the void left by their old jobs as business owners, a bit like a rock star having a comeback tour!

COME BACK TOUR

I also began to notice another type of person, a rare species who stood out from the crowd. These people seemed to be working from a very different, much more dynamic life plan. They often sold their businesses when they were still young and retired from their current working lives, where they had become bored, to try something new. They made big, bold decisions. Sometimes they migrated, sometimes they downsized. Sometimes they used my help to bring in people and systems to allow them to retire from their businesses, (effectively making themselves redundant) while keeping their asset and the income the business generated.

These people varied considerably in age. The common theme was that they made big, bold decisions and that their actions **bought them time.** Time to dance to their own tune, quality time to spend how they wanted. They were and are brilliant clients to work with, proactive and highly positive people following through on their goals and aspirations. People taking firm control of their lives and their destinies. **People writing their own stories.**

It became clear to me that far too many people put off retirement for too long because they felt they did not have enough money. Sadly as a result, they were often forced to sell their businesses due to ill health and when they did finally retire, their health issues impeded their quality of life preventing them from physically doing all the things they had been saving up for, the trip to Australia, that mid-week round of golf, becoming a missionary in Africa, or even opening a strip bar in Thailand (I have had some very colourful clients!) Tragically, some even died while still working and missed out on the retirement phase altogether. I would be instructed by their lawyer to sell their business to allow the money to be distributed to their estate.

As I saw these patterns repeated time and again, it became apparent to me that the conventional retirement model that they were conforming to was not serving many of these people very well. Like anything else, once you start to look for something you begin to notice it everywhere and increasingly, I saw the same thing happening outside of my professional life too. It was not just business owners, but people from all walks of life who also seemed to be falling into this trap of working too hard for too long and getting ill. With this in mind, I sought out further information on how I could better advise my clients to make more rounded, fully informed decisions about transitioning from full-time work to retirement and the best age to retire.

As I began to research retirement planning 'in the round' I was astonished to find that in a world awash with information, there was very little decent material available. Most resources targeted at people thinking about retirement planning seemed to fall into one of two camps.

It was either dry, factual or one dimensional information about **financial planning.** The kind of thing that your bank sends you about how much you need to save to provide you with a suitable retirement income.

On the other hand there were books, articles and papers on **how to slow down the ageing process.**

The problem with this readily available information is that it is almost exclusively written with an agenda to sell you a product or a service.

Fortunately, via my job I was blessed with a secret weapon, access to that rare breed of dynamic, non-conformist, inspiring people that I mentioned earlier. Those people who seemed to be working to their own plan, who successfully remodelled their lives to buy themselves quality time. The people I now call **Rock Star Retirees**. I made it my mission to study them as I wanted to share their secrets with my clients, and even more so, I wanted to **become** one of them!

Before I get ahead of myself, let's take a closer look at the conventional retirement and lifestyle advice we are being sold. I find this knowledge highly motivating. I for one do not want to be a sheep aimlessly following the flock. I am not prepared to be a passive victim being 'farmed' or 'harvested' for my money. I will not live my life following a system and a reality that is set by someone else's agenda to the detriment of my own. The question is will you, or are you ready to accept an alternative reality?

"Morpheus, it is time to wake up"
THE MATRIX, 1999[23]

---

[23] This is a brilliant film and if you have not already seen it, it is definitely one to add to your film bucket list.

D

Five years later, the price of oil was actually still lower than it was when he made his prediction.[24]

To be fair to pension companies and financial advisers, they really do have their work cut out. The truth is that no one can accurately predict future economics and the future value of your pension savings and investments.[25] Understand this and you understand that the current pension planning system, the mainstream model we are encouraged to follow, is at best limited, or at worst, fatally flawed.

Let's look at this in more detail, starting with the 'free' financial retirement information and associated planning tools that banks and pension companies offer. These days they are normally found online. Typically you are asked to enter the following information:

★ Your current age;
★ Your desired retirement age;
★ How much your existing pension pot and savings are worth;
★ Your desired monthly income when you retire.

You punch this into your computer or mobile phone and the app provides you with a **heavily disclaimed and caveated** amount that **you** need to save each month to **potentially** achieve this. Likewise, if you already have a pension, you will be used to similar annual projections about your existing scheme that come with your annual pension statement. These contain two key elements:

★ The current value of your pension;
★ A projection of what annual income this might give you at your chosen retirement date, normally based on the assumption that you will continue to pay in the same annual amount going forward as you paid in the current year.

---

[24] Source Business Insider UK. (Proof that even business Rock Stars can get financial predictions very badly wrong!)

[25] With the exception of those lucky enough to be on final salary pension schemes, where the amount you receive on retirement is pre-ordained and the funds raised to pay this are managed in a different way.

There are a number of problems with both of these financial projections and the methodology used. All of the projections are based on a very black and white situation whereby you hit a financial goal at a specified age. For all but the high rollers in the private sector, or those lucky enough to have historic, generous final salary pensions (such as long-serving policemen, teachers and UK civil servants) the numbers created by this model right now are extremely unfavourable or **downright unrealistic**. For the average person on an average annual salary, the amounts that need to be saved involve either working full time into your late 70s, or saving the vast majority of your income for most of your adult life, in effect, selling most of your life to buy a pension.

The calculations used for these projected values and income are complicated. They have to work on a number of variables that **no one** knows the answers to. These include:

★ How inflation will affect the value of your savings and investments,
★ What the compounded annual yield will be on your savings and investments, after charges and commissions from fund managers which often change
★ Variations in currencies relative to each other,
★ Compounded interest rates on any cash savings.

These complex and highly unpredictable economic variables are the reason that the pension projections you receive carry a **high**, **medium** and **low** level estimation of how your investment may perform. Stick with me, because this is where it gets interesting.

With these high, medium and low projections in your annual pension statement, it is quite normal for the projected annual yield from your pension savings to have a variance of over 90%! To put this into context, based on a 'typical' pensions industry approach, your projected income at your future retirement date might be somewhere between £12,500 per annum at the low end and £24,000 at the high end of expectation. So somewhere below the poverty line or somewhere reasonably comfortable! Basically, it is not much more than a lottery. Yet even with this humungous level of variance and unpredictability, there are a number of additional unknown variables not taken into consideration, which make things even more uncertain and unpredictable. These include:

★ The fact that there is no real thought about what your retirement might actually look like or what your annual financial needs will be when you retire. You could be in good health or house-bound. I know from my work as a business broker that many people never get to follow their dreams because their health deteriorates before they hit their planned retirement age. This is something that is impossible to accurately plan for.

★ How taxation will affect your investments and how your money will be taxed when you take it out of your retirement savings. This can be changed in the budget each year depending upon the whims and political and practical needs of the government of the day. This means that you can save earnestly for several decades based on certain tax efficient state-based initiatives and then the government can change the rules — **effective immediately**. In extreme cases when the state is short of cash to run the country it can even grab a chunk of your pension life savings. This happened in Argentina in 2008 when the Argentinian government took control of all privately held pension funds. The move was dressed up as an anti-corruption measure, but it was effectively a way for a cash-strapped government to get its hands on easy pickings and there was nothing the savers could do about it. Think this can't happen in the UK, US or Europe? If you take a look at the finances of pretty much ANY of the Western capitalist states there are some worrying early warning signs.

If you type 'retirement planning' into Google, you will be hit by a wall of results primarily focused on pension and financial planning. At the time of writing, this search phrase created over 34 million web-based articles on the subject context here in the UK. It is truly a massive global industry and a highly profitable one.

I don't want to get bogged down on the subject of the financial services industry in any great detail; however, it is a topic that does need to be covered. For some readers, this information will be new; for others it may already be well known.

Whatever the case, I hope that my presentation of the facts will prove highly motivating as a catalyst for some action towards you achieving your own Rock Star Retirement. **You see when it comes to the**

pensions industry, the house[26] always wins. When you pay into a pension you will normally be 'advised' to invest a large part of your hard earned savings into shares/equities. For the average person, you probably don't have the time or the expertise to select the appropriate stocks and shares, so the financial institutions provide a service for you. The way this works is that you choose one or more investment funds, or your independent financial adviser helps or does this for you. The fund manager gets paid a fee for managing your money and this normally takes the form of a percentage of the amount of money you invest.

Typically commissions for these managed funds are around 1.5%. So if you invest £10,000, the annual charge is £150 and if you invest £100,000 the annual charge will be £1,500. Yet in reality the fund manger is making the same decisions and doing the same amount of work. In my mind, this is a bit like paying someone to paint the front door of your house and then getting the same person to paint the front door of your neighbour's house. Now your house happens to be a detached four bedroom house while your neighbour's is a two bedroom semi. The doors are the same size, the contractor uses the same paint and exerts the same amount of time doing the painting, but you get charged twice as much as your neighbour simply because you have worked hard, been frugal and managed to buy a larger house! Fair? I don't think so.

But wait, it gets worse. The commission is paid whether or not the fund performs. In any other industry, if the person providing the service does not perform, then they don't get paid. If you genuinely hired someone to paint your door and they made a mess of it, would you still pay them when you end up having to strip off the paint and do the job again yourself? A bad decorator can cost you a day or two of your life, but at least you would not have to pay them for the inconvenience. Yet in the pension and mutual industry, fund managers are totally unaccountable. If they do a lousy job and lose you money, (meaning that you have to work longer and harder to top up your pension to the required level) they still get paid their commission. Investing in a poorly performing investment vehicle can genuinely cost you years of your life. And the reality is that most fund managers are not actually that good. Many

[26]   in the form of financial institutions and bank institutions and banks

studies have shown that once the high fees are factored in, it would have been better to have simply invested in a tracker fund. Tracker funds are simple lower cost investments that follow a range of investments — often the top 100 shares in any given market.

History repeating itself

Galling though it is, this is not a new phenomenon. Over 60 years ago Fred Schwed wrote a book entitled *Where are the customers' yachts?* The title was inspired by a story that is over a century old about a visitor to Manhattan, New York. Having admired the yachts owned by the financial advisers of Wall Street, acquired with money from giving financial advice to investors, he posed the rather rhetorical question. Where were the customers' yachts? Of course the answer was that there were virtually none. The point is as valid now as it was then. There is far more money in providing financial 'advice' and 'services' than there is in receiving financial advice, and the benefits achieved by following it. When it comes to financial services like savings and pensions, I repeat, **the house always wins.**

I need to make it clear that I don't have anything against financial advisers per-say; indeed I occasionally pay a trusted independent financial adviser to keep an eye on my own financial planning. (I'm sure she would tell you that I am a nightmare client because I always question her recommendations and don't always follow them.) However, the key message here is that traditional financial planning forms only one PART of your retirement planning — both before you 'retire' and during your 'retirement'. You just need to ensure that you don't rely **purely** on a large financial institution to look after your best interests. You need to take personal responsibility for educating yourself (like reading this book) and if you need to, find a financial adviser you can trust (mine happened to be a friend before they qualified as a financial adviser so I know that they have my best interests at heart and will tolerate my rather unorthodox approach.)

Now let's turn our attention away from finance to the other main body of work and resources currently focused around retirement. This is the multi billion pound 'health' industry. Take a closer look and the bulk of what is out there boils down to books, articles and soundbites from research papers on *how to slow down the ageing process.*

As a reward for your diligence in sticking with the previous, slightly technical financial section, we will now have a bit of fun with this subject, however, while the tone is light, the message is pertinent. The true significance may not dawn on you until later in the book as we begin to draw all of the lessons together.

The health-related information resources out there are generally product led pieces, or scientific papers frequently featuring sensationalised soundbites to attract the press and raise the profile of the lead scientist. More often than not, they promote a specific consumer product or interest group rather than actually providing practical help. You know the kind of thing about the anti-ageing properties of some recently discovered rain forest plant extract, miracle drug or super food. Here are some of my recent favourites to make you smile:

"The next new miracle super food: insects, scientists say"

"This thing is lightning in a bottle; it's a miracle flower to fight your fat"

"Coming to a supermarket near you: the pro-biotic olive"

This form of health-based marketing can be traced back to well before the 18th century with the peddling of snake oil and other amazing elixirs. A quick look through the advertising hall of fame (or perhaps shame) reveals some outrageous claims associated with some unlikely, but world class brands, at some point in their history being marketed for their health and medicinal properties.

The massive and enduring popularity of Coca Cola confirm that millions of consumers including myself find it delicious, but even for its most avid fans, its medicinal properties certainly appear rather spurious at best. Yet in the late 19th century Coca Cola was advertised as "*an ideal brain tonic*", and even a cure for impotence, with its creator American pharmacist John Pemberton describing it as "*a most wonderful invig-*

orator of sexual organs" *Undeniably a rousing slogan and a great product, but not THAT arousing!*

"A Mars a day helps you work, rest and play*"* is more subtle and for people of a certain age, holds significant nostalgia. However, less well remembered is the even bolder health-enhancing slogan that preceded it: **"Mars feeds you goodness three good ways."** These healthy living product virtues were definitely pushing the truth a bit. More recently, in 2008 the weight of regular Mars bars in the UK was reduced from 62.5 grams to 58 grams. Although not publicised at the time, when questioned, Mars claimed the change was designed to help tackle the obesity crisis in the UK. The company later confirmed that the real reason for the change was rising costs.[27]

The 1930s *"Guinness is good for you"* campaign definitely contained some Irish charm, with the claims that it promoted strength, relieved sleeplessness, aided digestion and contained iron, leading it to being fed to post-operative patients and blood donors for a while. Unbelievable, but true.

You could argue that marketing in those days wasn't quite so regulated, yet the modern advertising and marketing firms can trump even these.

Unsurprisingly this outrageous tongue in cheek advert for the brand POM Wonderful Juice was banned by the UK Advertising Standards Authority in 2009. POM's defence was that the claims were *"so exaggerated it could not possibly be taken seriously."* As they say, there is no such thing as bad publicity and I am sure that the publicity generated by the ban helped sales immensely.

You may think that is the pinnacle of insane marketing, but I have saved the best until last. You can now buy "low calorie" *Skinny Water* at major supermarkets. Apart from the Scottish 'fire water' variety, I have always been under the impression that water contains zero calories. It beggars belief doesn't it!

---

[27] Source Wikipedia

Key takeaways

The conventional life model of working to a fixed pre-ordained age, saving and investing money in a pension plan with the promise of a 'golden retirement' is not working for many people and the situation is likely to only get worse.

The traditional financial saving vehicles (pensions and saving schemes etc.) may be good investments, but they can also lose you money. They offer no guarantees that your pension target will be met. The only guarantee is that irrespective of their performance, the company administering your pension or savings scheme will always make money.

We had fun with some pretty extreme and spurious health claims from companies selling consumer products, but this is just the tip of the

iceberg. Much of what we are told and sold by the wealth and health industry is designed to make money for companies operating in the sector and is not necessarily the best advice or solution.

However, some people are following a different life model and utilising a different way of thinking. As a result they are thriving and living remarkably positive and fulfilling lives. I have dubbed them **Rock Star Retirees** and I have made it my life's work to study these people to find out how they do it. This book is the culmination of this work to date. I wrote it to share this knowledge with you so that you can apply it to your own life.

Why did I call this book the Rock Star Retirement Programme?

Firstly, the title is a nod to the fact that so many people retiring today come from the "rock 'n' roll generation", the post war baby boomers who grew up on a staple musical diet of rock and roll.

Secondly, the title is catchy, memorable and was created unashamedly with good marketing opportunities in mind. I believe that the lessons of this book can have such a positive impact on people's lives that naturally I want to share them with as many people as possible.

Thirdly, a rock star lifestyle is aspirational. It hints at irreverence to the normal life plan and to a more exceptional life. A life with more 'high points' and perhaps more passion; **a life less ordinary.** Follow the plan and this is exactly what you will get.

Finally, the title enables me to add a sense of humour to the subject matter to make it lighter and easier to read.

Can you really teach me to live like a rock star in retirement? What can I genuinely expect to get from this book?

My wife can do a mean Kate Bush impression and for a white guy I can play some passable blues riffs on a battered old Washburn guitar. My eldest son is almost grade one on the drums and my youngest son sings the theme tune from Frozen pretty well for a four year old. Perhaps my family's finest musical hour was when my sister won the 'Lower Flute Cup' at school nearly four decades ago. To maintain complete integrity, I should probably mention that she was the only one in the school that played the flute and disclose the fact that we never did manage to discover what happened to the 'Higher Flute Cup.' The Watson family's musical abilities pretty much end there.

I am also no Simon Cowell. I can't promise to help you to get "discovered" and then retire with the wealth of a rock star; at least not in the conventional, clichéd royalty and celebrity-fuelled millionaire sense. Yet like Simon Cowell, I have discovered a formula that works and is repeatable time and again to achieve success. Whatever your age, or level of talent, whatever your current circumstance, this book will provide you with the knowledge to live and retire the way you really want to.

How to use this book

Wow! We have covered a huge amount of information yet have not even really started. Long intros are no bad thing, we are in some very good company. In the Rock Star world some of the most iconic singles smashed the three minute song mould with unorthodoxly long introductions:

Dire Straits, Money for Nothing: 2 minutes, 4 seconds

Meat Loaf, Bat Out of Hell: 1 minute, 55 seconds

Iron Maiden, Fear of The Dark: 1 minute, 43 seconds

Guns N Roses, Paradise City: 1 minute, 21 seconds

This book is made up of ten lessons and presents a number of different Rock Star Retirement case studies. These range from the tranquil and sedate to the more risky and racy. They are real life illustrations of how ordinary and extraordinary people have followed their personal dreams to create a life that is rich and fulfilling for them; a life that works on their own terms. The beauty of the human race is that we are all unique. One man's meat is another man's poison. As a consequence, not all of the case studies may appeal to you. But they are provided to show you how other people have used the 10 principles to help them think outside the box and to shape their lives. They can help you realise you too can shape yours, to a life of your own making. Nothing would make me happier than if you become a Rock Star retiree case study too!

To ensure that you get the maximum benefits, please do complete the exercises.

A range of additional tools and resources to help you are also available at rockstarretirement.com

LESSON 1

SETTLE YOUR SCORES AND SEIZE THE DAY

WHY IT'S A GREAT TIME TO BE ALIVE

Well, people try to put us down.
Talkin' bout my generation.
Just because we get around.
Talkin' bout my generation.
The things they do look awful cold.
Talkin' bout my generation.
I hope I die before I get old.
Talkin' bout my generation.
My generation.
Why don't you all just fade away?
Talkin' bout my generation.
And don't try to dig what we all say

The Who — My Generation

T hrow away those rose tinted spectacles; it is time to neutralise that nostalgia! This is the best time to be alive in the whole history of the human race. It is also one of the best times to contemplate retirement, to be retired, or to be somewhere in between. Ignore the sensationalism and the conveyor belt of doom and gloom stories produced by the media. Put aside the subject of annuity rates and pensions, park the pessimism and take a look at the facts. For those of us lucky enough to be living in the Western World today, we need a little historic context to appreciate just how good we have it. While pension terms may not be quite as rosy as a decade or two ago, when you consider things from a wider perspective, we are incredibly lucky to be alive at this time.

You only have to look a few generations back to see that for the majority of our forefathers, there simply was no such thing as retirement. All but the rich simply worked until they could physically work no more. Back then, there were no social security hand-outs, no public health care schemes, no state safety nets and no other automatic benefits. Irrespective of your age, to afford basic food, shelter and clothing, you literally worked until you dropped. Those unable to work due to ill health were left to the mercy of charity. Most people's retirement planning consisted of having lots of children in the hope that some of their sons and daughters would support them and nurse them in their later years. **And that was if they managed to live to be old at all.**

Live Expectancy at Birth

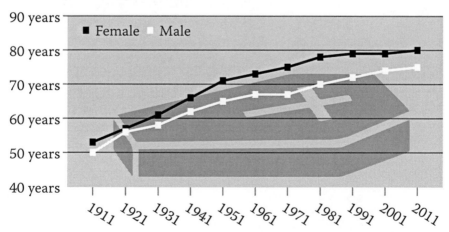

Source: https://ahundredyearsago.com/2011/08/09/life-expectancy-1911-and-2011/

Average life expectancy today is at the highest level since records began. The graph on page 34 illustrates just how favourable the current life expectancy statistics are compared with our ancestors. Indeed, if you are over 50 and if life expectancy had remained at the 1911 levels, chances are that you would already be dead, instead of being able to read this book! Although the speed of improvement in life expectancy is slowing down, modern medicine and healthcare services are still advancing rapidly meaning that the **quality of life** in later years looks set to continue to improve.

And the reasons to be cheerful about future retirement prospects go on.

Our modern democratic and capitalist society afford a lifestyle that our ancestors could never have dreamed of. We have more choices of restaurants, holiday destinations and leisure activities than ever before. Ironically while our ancestors biggest struggle was to feed themselves, we worry about obesity. Also our ancestors worried about surviving and feeding themselves in a wild and hostile environment yet we are concerned about animal welfare, environmental issues and our carbon footprint. How times have changed!

Modern Social Security in a Western society offers more support than ever. Where state support ends, groups of benevolent citizens take up the slack with food banks, soup kitchens and a multitude of voluntarily provided services.

The Internet has also opened up communication exponentially. There has never been so much readily available information and entertainment on demand, 24 hours a day, seven days a week, 52 weeks a year.

The mobile phone has provided us all with the ultimate personal, portable communications device. Via a Smart Phone, we can now do our banking, order takeaways, book a holiday and order shopping to be delivered to our door. We can even talk to our devices and they understand and talk back.

The demographics are moving increasingly in retirees favour in the Western world with older people forming both:

A significant social voting block in democratic societies, therefore able to protect social security rights in later age;

And a larger commercial audience for businesses which are increasingly tailoring their products to capitalise on the new mass market.

The robots are coming — in 2015 in Nagasaki, Japan, the Henn-na Hotel opened which is staffed 80–90% by robots. The humanoids perform reception duties, carry bags and even do cleaning duties. It is only a matter of time before this translates into care home androids and ultimately home-help robots too! So whatever your age, whether you just want to do less housework, or if you need much more assistance, autonomous robots look set to be an affordable way to provide this and in the near future will probably become as common as the family car!

Modern science now means that you can still enjoy sex well into your 70s, even your 80s and beyond! You may well be thinking "ewww" at this point, but you may well feel quite differently when you get there! Ageing used to mean a slow, steady decline in libido for women and in 'performance' for men. Now we have hormone replacement therapy (HRT) for women and the Viagra phenomenon for men. *How very Rock and Roll!*

The law is likely to become more on the side of older people too. Our societies have undergone a number of major battles during their continuing evolution:

The battle against class and patronage—enabling people to access education and jobs not based upon the wealth or social standing they were born into but allowing them to rise through society based on merit and hard work (or reality TV);

The battle of the sexes — giving women the vote and equal opportunities in the workplace and in government;

The battle against racism, giving people of all colour and races equal rights within the law;

The battle for a secular society where the state does not dictate or enforce a common religion, but the right of the individual to worship if they so wish.

I fully expect that in the coming decades, as society further develops and adapts to an ageing population, that the next big development will be for society to deal better with age discrimination and for cultural attitudes to become more positive and embracing to the elderly. After all, age really is just a number and one 67-year-old can be very different from another. In many historic cultures and societies older people were highly respected and revered. The hope that in a decade or two the wisdom of the elders may once again become a prized asset is no more ridiculous than the thought not so long ago that women might one day serve on the front line in the military, or that same sex marriages would become legal.

Taking into account all of these factors: higher life expectancy, better healthcare and an improved quality of later life, as well as technology advances, more affluent and benevolent societies, plus more consumer choice and likely social and legal evolution to support older citizens, the prognosis for your later years is very good indeed. You just need the knowledge to know how to harness these favourable conditions. Wherever you are in your thinking now and whatever your personal circumstances, there is so much to be optimistic about.

Every time I listen or watch the news or read a paper it's all doom and gloom. So if as you say, the world is such a great place to live in, why does it not feel like it?

Media channels, supported by an infrastructure of super-fast global communications, are both a blessing and blight. Like never before we can in real-time get insights into things that are happening on the other side of the world. However, listen to the typical international daily news bulletin and it will be dominated by the depressing topics of violent crime, terrorism, war and natural disasters. Social media too seems to be beginning to follow this trend, although not yet to the same extent. Now consider your own **direct experience** of the world on any normal day as you go about your day-to-day business in the real world. What do you see with your own eyes, what do you hear with your own ears? Does it really reflect what you see on the news? If you are being honest, then I very much doubt it!

The problem with modern news channels is that the ratio of bad news stories to good has become ridiculously distorted. The reality is that probably around 80% of people are decent and only around 20% questionable. For every major crime, or natural disaster, reported on the television, there are many thousands of unreported good news stories, tales of random acts of kindness, people giving up their time freely and willingly to help others from the goodness of their hearts. Think about it and look around you. Most people are good, the planet we inhabit is mostly benign and accommodating, however, it is just that the bad news events are amplified and sensationalised by the media and if you let them in without putting them into context, they will invade your consciousness to a disproportionate level.

People on a normal retirement journey tend to spend more of their days listening to, or reading, the news. It is a natural way to fill some of the time vacated by their withdrawal from work. However, with the current news format being so negative, this can begin to turn someone previously optimistic into someone rather more pessimistic. Further on I will share some specific strategies for maintaining a sensible perspective and ensuring that you maintain a positive and healthy world view. For now, the key thing to remember is that most of the time the immediate world that we inhabit day to day is a pretty good place to be. Good and bad things have and will always happen. It is undeniable that we have it far better than all of our ancestors and predecessors and we owe it to them to realise this and enjoy the opportunities we have been blessed with.

"The old have reminiscences of what never happened"
SAKI, REGINALD

Recognising nostalgia for the illusion that it is

Do you remember when you were young, attractive and in your so-called prime? Do the memories of your youth and your past glories fill you with nostalgia? The scary thing is that, all too often, I hear people in their mid to late 20s talking like this. Left uncontrolled and unchallenged, our memories of the past can become distorted and unhelpful. Without conscious questioning, how the brain automatically recalls and presents the past can actually become highly misleading. If you think about your parents' generation, you will definitely see evidence of this. You may well exhibit some of the traits yourself.

Some typical phrases relating to this type
of rose tinted nostalgia include:
"They don't make them like they used to …"
"In the good old days …"
"Back in the day …"
"When I was a lad …"
(Best said in a Monty Pythonesque Yorkshire accent)

Many people fall into the "grass is always greener" syndrome and romanticise about the past as some sort of golden age. Although it is great to recall positive memories, it is also important not to dwell on them in an unbalanced or even downright false historical context.

With our youthful physical strength and beauty there was also often a beast; we may have been more attractive and have had more energy but we were also often more shallow, vain, selfish, insecure and needy. Don't forget this and fall into the trap of looking back with those overly rose tinted spectacles — come on now, I asked you to throw them away back on page 36!

No more excuses: time to park the past

As we get older, many people increasingly focus on the regret of missed opportunities. I see this frequently when I am helping people to prepare exit plans prior to the sale of their businesses:

"If only I had known then what I know now ..."

"With hindsight, I would have made some very different choices"

For these people, recalling the past can fill them with melancholy about what might have been if they had done things differently. For example, if they had worked harder, chosen a different career path, taken a year out, gone to university, started a family earlier, spent more time with their children in their precious formative years, been more careful about eating and exercise, or perhaps emigrated.

For a while, I pondered on the best way to deal with these regrets. What advice could I offer my clients to provide comfort and a means for them to look forward with more hope and optimism? Eventually I plucked up the courage to actively begin to seek the answers. The obvious place to look was my cohort of rock star retirees who seemed so happy in their skins and with their focus constantly looking forwards rather than back. I wanted to know what their secret was. On investigation, it quickly transpired that it was not anything to do with them having had a perfect life, or an uncanny knack of making perfect decisions. On the contrary, they all confessed to having made loads of mistakes. They had also all had their normal quota of bad things happen to them. Their secret weapon is the logic to accept that what is done is done and that until someone invents a time machine, what happened in the past, stays in the past. So they give themselves a bit of time to come to terms with things, dust themselves off, set a new course and never look back! Their message is pretty unanimous:

"Life is short and we never know how long we have got. There is too little time for dwelling on past wrongs or regrets, you have to seize the day today. One door closes, another opens, there is so much life to be lived. Your life is what you make it"

*"Some people are old at 18 and
some are young at 90...
time is a concept that humans created"*
YOKO ONO

Time to focus on the present and look to the future with optimism

As the Rock Star Retirees have shown, the only thing we can influence is our behaviour and actions right now. How we act in the present defines both the here and now as well as the future. We can't choose what events life throws at us, we can only choose how we react to them.

Whether you are 25 or 85, right now you are the youngest you are ever going to be — FACT. It is therefore important to embrace what you **have**, not what you **had**.

Age is just a number, a state of mind. It is up to you to choose which equation you apply to it. As your age grows, you can choose whether to multiply your opportunities, or divide them.

"You can't stop the waves,
but you can learn to surf on them"

ORIGIN UNKNOWN

There are countless examples of people who achieved amazing things later in life:

50+ Francisco Pizarro: Quinquagenarian Conquestador

Born in the 1470's Francisco Pizarro was in his fifties when he finally conquered Peru in 1530. This was an incredible feat, men had a far shorter life expectancy in those days and his was not a comfortable life. Born illegitimately, he nevertheless pushed himself to succeed within the Spanish conquests of the "New World". He was driven by word of the Inca riches and despite two failed attempts and having his support withdrawn, he petitioned King Charles I successfully and was given funding and the right to claim the lands in his name. He defeated Emperor Atahualpa's army in November 1532 following the bloody battle of Cajamarca in which the Inca's were defeated. Regardless of how you feel about the Spanish conquests, there is no doubt that this man gave no thought to his advancing years as he took on the might of a hostile Peru.

60+ Colonel Sanders: sexagenarian businessman

Harland Sanders, better known as Colonel Sanders, was well over 60 when he made it big with Kentucky Fried Chicken. Before then, he simply sold chicken and other food at a food outlet located in a service station in Kentucky. When Interstate 75 was built it diverted traffic away from his restaurant and his business was close to failing. Forced to adapt, he hit the road and pitched his unique recipe over 1,000 times before someone decided to give him a chance. With investment secured he went on to found the now international KFC fast food chain.

70✚ Peter Roget: creative peak in his 70s

Roget showed us that it is never too late to make significant inventions and contributions to human culture and improvement. He came up with the concept of the famous Thesaurus at the age of 73. The story goes that suffering from OCD, the only thing that would calm him down was making random lists. In the end, he simply started on the infinite project of creating a list of synonymous words. Roget's Thesaurus of English Words and Phrases' has never been out of print since its initial appearance and it has now been adopted into modern word processors.

80✚ Jessica Tandy: winner of the best actress Oscar aged 80

Starring alongside the legendary Morgan Freeman, British, Brixton-born octogenarian actress Jessica Tandy gave the screen performance of her life in the classic 1989 multi-award winning film Driving Miss Daisy. (If you have not seen it yet, this is one to add to your movie bucket list. It is a timeless masterpiece.)

90✚ Harry Bernstein: published and celebrated author in his 90s

His critically acclaimed 2007 memoir 'The invisible wall: a love story that broke barriers,' was started when Bernstein was 93 and published in 2007, when he was 96. The loneliness he encountered following the death of his wife, Ruby, in 2002, after 67 years of marriage, was the catalyst for Bernstein to begin work on his book.

100✚ Faujah Sing: centenarian marathon man

In October 2011 at the age of 100, Indian Faujah Sing completed the Toronto waterfront marathon to become the oldest man to finish a full 26.2 mile marathon. Astonishingly, Mr Sing only came to competitive running at the age of 89 after losing his wife and son. There is a very current female role model too, Canadian Harriette Thompson, who became the oldest woman to complete a marathon when she crossed the finish line at San Diego's Rock 'n' Roll Marathon in June 2015. She was 92 years and 93 days old.

As these amazing people demonstrate, **age is not an excuse**. Everyone has unfinished business: wake up and smell the coffee!

When I talk to older people about this the initial response tends to be along the lines of:

"But I am not as physically fit as I used to be, so how can my opportunities increase rather than decrease? How can I possibly live life to the full when my body is just not up to it?"

If you are really thinking along these lines, I strongly urge you to watch 'A history of everything,' the story of Professor Stephen Hawking. He suffered from motor neuron disease which gradually paralysed him. His condition was diagnosed when he was 21 and at the time the doctors gave him two years to live. Did he accept this prognosis and just give up? Did he hell! "Fiercely independent and unwilling to accept help or make concessions for his disabilities.[28]" Professor Hawking preferred to be regarded as "a scientist first, popular science writer second, and, in all the ways that matter, a normal human being with the same desires, drives, dreams, and ambitions as the next person" The rest is history. Despite becoming wheelchair-bound and severely paralysed, having to talk via a computer, Professor Hawking made major advances in theoretical physics.

My childhood hero, British World War II fighter pilot Douglas Bader provides another brilliant reality check. In 1931 also at the age of 21 and just a year into his flying career, while attempting a series of acrobatic manoeuvres at an air show, Bader crashed his plane and was critically injured. He survived, but lost both legs below the knee. Did he accept that his best days were behind him and spend the rest of his days in a

---

[28] White & Gribbin 2002

convalescence home, living off an airforce pension and feeling sorry for himself? Not a chance!

His story is even more inspiring when you consider that back then prosthetic leg technology was extremely basic, there were no made to measure super hi-tech lightweight carbon fibre limbs.

Despite having crude and uncomfortable wooden legs he taught himself to walk again. Not content to live off an RAF invalidity pension he made up his mind that he was going to fly again. Having recovered his strength and mobility, he retook flight training, passed his check flights and requested reactivation as a pilot. Although there were no regulations applicable to his situation, he was retired against his will on medical grounds. He did not accept this situation and continued to lobby the RAF top brass for reinstatement. His persistence eventually paid off and the opportunity came after the outbreak of the Second World War in 1939. With a shortage of experienced pilots he finally persuaded the RAF selection board to reconsider his case and was accepted as a pilot.

His amazing story does not end here. During the "Battle of Britain" he became a popular cult hero. He is credited with shooting 20 enemy planes down, four shared victories, six 'probables', one shared probable and 11 enemy aircraft damaged. He was promoted to Squadron leader and was instrumental in pioneering RAF cutting edge flying strategies and tactics.

In August 1941 he was himself shot down over German occupied France where he was captured and sent to a prisoner of war camp. But you could just not keep this man down! Despite his disability he gave his German captors as much trouble as he had previously the RAF top brass when badgering them for flying reinstatement. He made a number of escape attempts, eventually being sent to the notorious and ultra-secure Colditz Castle. The Germans eventually reverted to taking his legs away at night to prevent further escape attempts.

He remained at Colditz until April 1945 when the camp was liberated by the United States Army. After the war he received numerous honours, the pinnacle of which was a knighthood from the Queen.

Douglas Bader's incredible story is told in the book Reach for the Sky. It is well worth a read. If you are pressed for time the quicker option is to track down the film of the same name. It is an oldie [1956], but this incredible true story does not need modern CGI to be entertaining or relevant.

The main theme you need to take away from this is that whether you are 21 or 81 and your body can't do what it used to do, with the right mind-set, you can still reach new heights. Stop making excuses in your head!

The final objection I often hear when I present this optimistic outlook is that the people I cite are all exceptional, ultra-talented or ultra-determined *"one in a million"* kind of people; they are not representative. In some ways this is right however, this is why they make such great stories. There are literally tens of millions of far less famous, but still impressive, examples of people who have continued to live life to the full and remain open minded, flexible and willing to try new things. Here a few examples from my own life to give you a feel for the sort of things I mean.

★ My mum: when she became too ill to go to work she took up painting. She reinvented herself and found something she could fill her time with at home doing something constructive. She went on to become a successful local artist selling her paintings for many hundreds of pounds each.

★ My mum and dad: despite various health issues they went for their first hot air balloon flight at the combined age of 130. I have to confess that I bought them the tickets, but all credit to them for rising to the challenge. The flight took place on the borderline of safe wind speeds and had to be cut short as the balloon was nearly blown out to sea. As they made an emergency landing, the basket clipped the chimney of a house and landed rather heavily. At the time there were some comments about whether this was part of my Rock Star Retirement Planning to obtain an early inheritance!

★ Friends at my local running club: some are in their mid to late 60s who are beating people a third of their age in half-marathons and

10k races (someone forgot to tell them they are not supposed to be able to do this!)

★ My neighbours Mark and Lyndsey who decided to 'up sticks' with their two young children and emigrate to Australia at the age of nearly 50.

★ My sister who was made redundant in her early 40s and went on to seize the day by setting up her own consultancy company (she never looked back!)

If you take the time to think about your own friends, family and acquaintances, I am sure you can think of examples of inspiring people who have risen to challenges — big and small — in order to change the status quo and improve their lot in life, despite their circumstances. Take a minute or two to think about this. If the exceptional people like Douglas Bader, Stephen Hawking and the normal people like my family and friends can rise to the challenge and make changes to their lives for the better, despite their health issues, then whatever your age, current health and financial circumstances, why can't you?

If you honestly can't think of any inspirational examples in your own life, then it's time to shake things up and make some new friends and acquaintances. More about this later.

Circumstances mean nothing.
Limitations mean nothing.
Obstacles mean nothing.
It all comes down to you!

LESSON 1 SUMMARY

Whatever your current age and means, take time to appreciate what you do have right now. Remember that the outlook for diet, life expectancy, healthcare, leisure and wellbeing are the most positive they have ever been in the history of humanity.

News channels paint a distorted picture of the world. Good and bad things have, and will, always happen. However, for those of us lucky enough to be living in the Western world today, we really have never had it so good. It is important to put things into context.

Don't fall into the trap of over-romanticising your youth. Embrace getting older, it is not going to go away. Today you are as young as you are ever going to be again. Don't obsess over your past youthful looks. Learn to love and accept yourself as you are now. Some things were better when you were younger, some are better now, while others will be better in the future. Make the most of the fantastic opportunities that our current society offers.

Holding onto, and dwelling on past regrets achieves nothing. Don't use past experiences as an excuse to stop you doing things in the present. The future starts right now. Time is precious.

Growing older is mandatory; growing up is optional. Age is just a number, don't use it as an excuse to limit your expectations of what you can yet achieve. There are plenty of role models out there to show you that it is possible to run your first marathon at 89, launch a new business at 73, or learn a new skill at any age.

If you open your eyes and search them out, you will find that beyond the 'celebrated' success stories from famous people, there are plenty of amazing people in your local community, family or social peer groups. These people will be quietly living their lives to the maximum, trying new ideas and in the context of their ages and circumstances, doing some quite extraordinary things.

Sickness and decreasing physical abilities may make some things unachievable, but as one door closes, another opens. Celebrate what you have, don't rue what you don't have.

Time flies. It is time to seize the day!

ROCK STAR RETIREMENT MANTRA:

"Remember that guy that gave up?
Neither does anybody else!"

LESSON 2

50 SHADES OF GREY

UNDERSTANDING THE TRAP AND PLANNING YOUR ESCAPE

[DISCOVERING ALTERNATIVE APPROACHES TO RETIREMENT & LIFE PLANNING]

Billy don't like it living here in this town
He says the traps have been sprung long before he was born
…It's a rat trap Billy but you're already caught ….
But you can make it if you want to
or you need it bad enough …

…In this town Billy says "everybody tries to
tell you what to do"
In this town Billy says "everybody says you gotta follow
rules …Walk don't walk
Talk don't talk"
Hey Billy take a walk with me …
"It's a rat trap ….. and we've been caught …"

RAT TRAP — Boomtown Rats, 1978

Throughout the rest of this book you are going to meet a number of other people, providing more case studies to illustrate real life examples of different approaches to life and life planning. A number of these people have already retired in the traditional sense, but none have done so using the traditional planning routes. Before we look more deeply at how they did this, let's consider the plight of Frank again. I have interacted with, and know, lots of people like Frank. People who often as early as their mid-30s become so sick of their everyday existence that all they can think about is how much better life will be when they retire, simply because it represents a departure from the rat race trap they have fallen into.

The seeds of their problems were planted in their most formative years. Our lives in the Western world are mapped out from an early age. We start school at four and although we are initially allowed the freedom to dream and role play about becoming an astronaut or a doctor, a fireman or a train driver, very quickly our thinking becomes institutionalised into a very formulaic life plan.

As we mature and begin to expand our view of the world, we are then brainwashed by the media and current popular culture to think of success in terms of an incredibly limited two-dimensional set of metrics: **money and status.** The focus is on a **career** rather than a **vocation**, the social status of the job title and what house or car the pay packet will help us achieve. The forward thinker may also look into what sort of pension plan and benefits the job carries. All good and important stuff, the kind of things that your financial planner and bank manager would emphasise. Yet there is one, massive, glaring omission. Far too little time is spent getting a proper understanding about the reality of the **day to day existence** of performing the job and how happy (or otherwise) it will make us **feel** while doing it.

For the average employed person in the UK, contractual working hours take up roughly 50% of our waking hours. Sometimes we have to work extra, doing paid or unpaid hours, covering for colleagues, during very busy times, or perhaps when a project deadline is looming. Our jobs can encroach on our lives during our free-time too. We saw this when we met Frank for the first time. It was a Sunday evening and he was already thinking about Monday, dreading going back to work.

For those lucky enough to love what they do to earn a living, this is not a problem. Take your average real life rock star and there is a genuine blurring of the lines. Strumming away on a guitar and writing a new song is both work and play. Unfortunately rock stars and Rock Star Retirees are in the minority.[29] For most people, there is a massive void between the hopes and aspirations of their chosen career and the day to day reality of living it.

Sadly, this perception versus reality phenomena is all too apparent for many within the field in which I specialise, the optical sector. Bright young students are primarily drawn to training to be an optometrist by the medical and clinical aspects of the role. Their expectation is that the job will be rather like that of a doctor, but with a niche focus on the eye. However, the day-to-day reality for the average optician is radically different. Firstly there is the working environment. If you have had your eyes tested in the UK recently you should be able to picture it. A typical testing room is around eight square metres. Optometrists really do operate in a tiny bubble. A claustrophobic, box of a room furnished by equipment for testing eyes; equipment which comes in any shade that you can possibly imagine, as long as it is beige.[30]

To make matters worse, the majority of each eye examination is conducted in the dark, meaning that testing rooms either have no windows, or that the windows are permanently boarded up, or covered by blackout blinds. As a result of this, the majority of an optometrist's working life is spent without exposure to natural light. Admittedly, this is not as harsh as working down an 18th century coal mine, but you have to agree that this is not an ambient working environment, or a daily backdrop that will make your soul sing with the joy of life!

Then there are the commercial pressures. In the UK, the reality is that the average opticians business makes very little money from testing eyes. The cost of the premises, lighting, heating, insurance and staffing required to conduct the 20–40 minute sight test are frequently greater than the price charged to the patient (or the NHS) for the sight test. In

---

[29] Although I sincerely hope that this book will improve the statistics for the latter.

[30] Arguably the world's most drab colour

most instances, the sight test is actually a loss-making exercise! Therefore, to make money, opticians need to sell glasses as this is where they can actually make a profit. As a result, opticians are under pressure to fit in as many sight tests as possible into their working days which means they have to rush through the clinical bit to maximise the selling opportunities. Success is mostly measured, not in terms of their clinical expertise, but in their capability as salespeople. Quite a departure from the 'eye doctor' job that the optometrist thought they were originally signing up for.

In recent years, the poor suffering optician's plight has become even more personally hazardous and stressful. Eyes have sometimes been described as "the windows to the soul." From a medical and, optometry perspective, a more up to date description is probably "the window to the overall health of a person."

In the 21st century, the eye test has gone way beyond a simple vision test, it now encompasses a full examination of the health of the eye.

In addition to core eye health, optometrists now have to look out for and think about a number of other symptoms that can present during the eye test which may indicate health problems elsewhere in the patient's body. Eye tests can now detect symptoms of numerous other conditions, of which an early diagnosis can quite literally save a life: pituitary tumours, brain tumours, diabetes, hypertension and high cholesterol to name a few. The optometrist is responsible for referring the patient to a doctor or a specialist if any indicators of other potential health problems are detected. As the 2016 Honey Rose court case illustrated, resulting in a criminal charge against the 35-year-old practitioner, optometrists are personally liable should they fail to pick up any such symptoms. More and more is being asked clinically, while less and less time and remuneration is being given to optometrists to carry out these extra checks and responsibilities due to commercial concerns.[31]

---

[31] The good news is that it does not have to be like this, as well as helping opticians to escape – by helping them to sell their businesses, I also teach them how to operate differently (so they don't have to escape!)

I highlighted the optical sector because this is a field I know particularly well. However, this perception of what a job entails versus the day-to-day reality of performing it happens in so many other business sectors and careers. Indeed, for many people, the situation is significantly worse. My wife spent the first 20 years of her career as a primary school teacher. She and the vast majority of her colleagues genuinely love teaching and interacting with children, it truly is a vocation.

Externally, many people perceive that teachers have an easy life with short working hours conducted in a positive nurturing environment, not to mention the legendary long school holidays. Yet in most schools in England, the classroom 'teaching' element — the vocational reason student teachers sign up in the first place — represents only half of the role. In the UK, education has become highly politicised. Although budgets have been squeezed, expectations of teaching staff have increased dramatically.

As a result teachers now have to put in huge numbers of unpaid hours, creating bespoke lesson plans and filling out endless paperwork to comply with the latest Westminster-driven initiative. My wife got to the point where she had so little time to spend with our own children that she decided enough was enough. Before she retired from teaching (at the age of 42), it was not uncommon for her to be working past midnight most mid-week nights and having to work for one full day of the weekend. As a couple, we were fortunate in that when we talked things over and reviewed our budget, we found that if we were careful with our money, my earnings would be enough to cover all of our basic outgoings. But what if this is not the case?

In the first chapter, I mentioned our friends and neighbours Mark and Lindsey, who in their late 40s moved their family to Australia in search of a better life. Like my wife Julie, Lindsey was a primary school teacher. She also loved working with children, but she too was being ground down by the huge administrative burden, the long unpaid hours and the politics in education. At the age of 46, she too retired from her teaching post, but in a very different way. Lindsey did not stop working, instead her retirement led to a very different change in her day-to-day reality.

After significant research and with support from her husband Mark, she found a job in a school in Melbourne, Australia. The pay was better, but more importantly the day-to-day reality of the job was far superior. A combination of better management, a more positive culture, smaller class sizes, more sophisticated IT resources and less politics meant that she was able to focus on the part she loved — teaching. Since 2010, Melbourne has won the Economist magazine's "most liveable world city" for six years in a row. Based on this and other research, they figured it would be a good move for all of the family. Having visited them very recently, I can confirm that they live in a beautiful place and are building a great new life for themselves with a far superior quality of living in the absence of the stresses which Lindsey's job previously put her under. And while getting used to having a barbecue in beachwear rather than a traditional Christmas turkey dinner in a yuletide jumper is proving hard for them to get used to, it is looking like a very shrewd move for the whole family!

So before spending the next two or three decades marking time in an unsatisfactory existence waiting for the traditional retirement dream; instead of wondering where your next holiday escape is going to be, or fixating each week solely on the weekend, on life outside of work, how about following Mark and Lindsey's lead by creating a life that **you don't need to escape from** at a much earlier stage? It does not have to be quite as dramatic as emigrating to the other side of the world, but it does involve changing the reality and happiness of day-to-day living and thinking.

Our next and most detailed case study so far is a great example of how to escape the trap of a deeply unsatisfactory career to shape the way you want your life to be.

ROCK STAR RETIREMENT CASE STUDY

From board room to boiler room, a contrarian life-changing success story

There is no denying it. Going from successive executive jobs for companies listed on the NASDAQ and FTSE 250, to running your own chimney sweeping business, is a highly unusual journey.

Far too many people moan about their present situation but fail to act to implement the necessary changes. However, John (pictured above) found his sanity and happiness by forgoing the status symbols associated with a successful career and became a chimney sweep. For both him and for his wife, this was far from expected, but they could not be happier!

John's career journey: from A to B to being FREE

John was a founder member of the Starbucks UK management team, responsible for carrying out a massive expansion programme, starting in 1998. Over an 11-year period, he was personally responsible for opening 120 new outlets as the company went from 47 coffee shops to over 700.

His role was very demanding, but he was young, had lots of time, few commitments and was happy to give it his all.

However, as we know, expansion cannot go on forever and he was eventually made redundant as part of an urgent cost-cutting exercise at the height of the recession when the store opening programme was mothballed.

He was treated well and received a decent severance package. Indeed, when talking about Starbucks, John's tone and body language illustrate a justifiable pride in his achievements and a continuing fondness for the company in which tellingly, he still owns shares.

This happy nostalgia quickly evaporates as his thoughts turn to memories of his subsequent employed work, in particular his final executive post at a national brewery and pub chain.

This was clearly a dark time in his life. He did not buy into the corporate culture which he describes as "Foolishly obsessed with the short-term share price, rather than the bigger picture and the long-term health of the business and its products and personnel."

He hated the corporate bullshit and had serious moral concerns about some aspects of what he was expected to do.

He was driving over 800 miles a week and the hours were hideously long. He frequently received urgent phone calls at unsociable hours. These intrusive calls came at random times of day and night, often encroaching on weekends and he was expected to drop everything and jump into a car to spend as long as was necessary to troubleshoot the problems.

Despite working really hard, he never received recognition, reward or time off in lieu for working way beyond his contractual obligations. He also had a wife and two young daughters, but little quality time to truly enjoy a normal family life.

"The catalyst for change", he says "was getting fed up of hearing myself moan. I thought to myself that if I felt that way about myself ...God help my friends and family! I hardly got to see them and when I did, I was tired, stressed and totally miserable to be around."

Something clearly had to give.

Mental emancipation from an altered mindset

Recognition of a need for change is the crucial starting point, but how and where do you begin the process of getting yourself out of a rut?

For John, it began with a heart-to-heart with his wife. He felt immeasurably better once he had told her how he was feeling and that he desperately wanted to break away from the miserable corporate world he found himself trapped in. She was surprisingly receptive to his radical thinking and unwaveringly supportive. They had saved John's redundancy pay from Starbucks and his wife even suggested that he quit his job immediately and use this to live off until he found his new calling.

At the age of 39, with the full backing of his family, John began to research new avenues. However, he was unwilling to part with his hard-earned savings so easily and so he was not prepared to quit until he had alternative plans in place.

An interesting side effect John mentioned when I interviewed him is a common theme I observe from those people in a difficult present reality, but who are resolved to be positive and change things. It's a feeling of relief and emancipation. During the initial research phase, things became more bearable at work. The day job remained the same, it was his mindset that had altered. Empowered by the hope of a brighter future somewhere else, he began to wrestle back control from his employers.

★ He no longer felt like a wage slave.

★ The job was no longer everything.

★ He no longer lived in fear.

He began to speak his mind to his bosses and to say no to some of the non-contractual unpaid hours. While it was not a good long-term 'employee career strategy' and he understood that it might not be tolerated for long, it bought him more much needed extra time to follow his new passion of making a better future for himself, while still being paid.

John and his wife spent all of their available spare time trawling the internet and reading books, often long after the children had gone to bed.

However, John held no long supressed vocational desires and there was nothing obvious jumping out at the couple. They started out with an almost totally blank canvas — probably the hardest of all places to begin to plan. But they were committed to action and they persisted. Their initial foundation was a simple list of "wants" and "don't wants" for a new job or career. Over time, this evolved into a list of non-negotiable requirements:

★ John wanted to be fully accountable for his actions, but to be immune from other people's complex agendas, for example company and inter-departmental politics.

★ He wanted there to be a direct link between the amount of effort and time he put into his job and the reward he got out of it.

★ He wanted a degree of working time flexibility to allow him to spend more time with his family, go to the children's plays and class assemblies.

★ He wanted to spend less time driving.

★ Having been used to a decent remuneration package, he needed a career path that had the potential to provide a similar standard of living, but he was prepared to fall back on his redundancy savings and earn a lower amount in the short-term 12 to 18 months.

It quickly became obvious that John needed to work for himself to stay true to these non-negotiables. He needed to either start a business, or buy an existing business so that he could be his own boss.

As the thought process evolved, he then began a more detailed review of his career experiences. Obtaining a clearer picture of the specific aspects of what he was good at and equally important, what he was not good at, as well as things he enjoyed and things he hated.

He concluded that:

★ He was definitely a "people person" and enjoyed interacting with lots of different people on a regular basis.

★ He was practical more than creative. His strengths lay in executing plans through to successful outcomes, rather than inventing new ideas and systems from scratch.

★ He had thoroughly enjoyed the experience of building up Starbucks UK and the prospect of building up another business excited him.

★ His family commitments and financial situation meant that he had no more than 18 months' worth of savings to tide him over. And his new business or career needed to provide him with a similar revenue level as his old one within 18 months of starting.

After three months, this evaluation process had begun to lead him down the franchised business route. He liked the idea of having a proven system to follow, but with the satisfaction of creating and building the business up from the ground, just like he had done at Starbucks. Only this time the business would be wholly owned by him. Having managed and dealt with the problems of employing staff, he was also increasingly drawn to a more simple business, where he was both the brains and the brawn and did not have to rely on anyone else. This further narrowed down his options.

John can't quite put his finger on what drew him to specifically choosing a chimney sweeping franchise. He admits that it was totally random, but says that it just kept popping up on his internet research and ticking all of the boxes for his non-negotiables, as well as his wants and needs.

In my experience of observing, interviewing and working with people making significant life-changing decisions, there are common patterns. John's feeling of liberation and freedom having made that initial emotional **decision** to seek change was very much to form. Another almost bolt-on certainty is that, having honed down the options and decided upon the front runner, there is then a tendency to delay properly committing to the likely solution. However, there is almost always a final trigger that pushes the person to pick up the phone. This was also the case for John.

The catalyst for him was "an hour and a half circular conversation with my boss about setting targets that I felt were delusional. He was too far removed from the coalface and was happy to just follow the corporate direction rather than face reality. As ever it would be me left to pick up the pieces when staff called in sick with stress. I came home fuming and vowed that this was the final straw. That evening I took the plunge and spoke to the franchisor for the first time." The rest as they say is history.

Happy days

John has been successfully running his own business since August 2012. He executed the start-up plan flawlessly and won the franchisee of the year award for his organisation in his second year of trading, repeating this achievement twice further. The award was based on financial performance, delivery of service of the brand and positive input to the overall franchise group.

John's remuneration is now much the same as of his previous job, but he works significantly less hours. The quality of his life is "immeasurably better." Although he still gets the odd out of hours calls, these days he doesn't mind too much as they come from customers who appreciate the value of his time and are prepared to pay for it.

He manages his own diary and is very much his own man. He loves being his own boss and the fact that the buck stops with him. He is responsible for whether he is having a good day, a good month or a good year. He enjoys the interactions with his customers. They come from a broad mix of backgrounds, including high flyers and other business owners, who I suspect are frequently surprised by his capacity to talk about and even provide advice on their businesses at a very high level! In a similar vein, he also relishes networking with other local business owners and having an influence on the future direction and strategy of the parent franchise brand.

John sees his children and wife a lot more and by his own admission is less grumpy. With more time to spend on things of his own choosing, he is now a school governor at his daughters' school. A few years ago this would have been unthinkable.

If you are shallow enough to measure a person purely on their job title, and the car they drive, then I concede that John's career change has been a major regression. But if you measure it on almost any other metric then this cannot be viewed as anything other than a resounding success: a move from a vanity job to a sanity job. John has escaped the rat race and his destiny, wealth and happiness lie in his own hands. *Many congratulations John on becoming a successful Rock Star Retiree!*

As someone who has spent the majority of his working life helping people to sell their businesses, it would be remiss of me not to also mention the other practical benefit of John starting up his own successful business. He has created a saleable asset that when he feels the time is right he will be able to sell for a nice five-figure sum. You can't sell a job, but a decent lifestyle business almost always carries a reasonable transfer value. In practice this means that, if he so desires, John will be able to sell his business and afford to take a couple of years out without working. Alternatively the money could be used to enable John to retire in a conventional sense a good few years earlier than he would otherwise have been able to.

So other than 'traditional' retirement planning, what other options are there if you genuinely don't want to work anymore?

This book is about the concept of retirement in many contexts. As already outlined, if you follow the black and white conventional thinking of the average financial planner then you are playing Russian roulette with your life. There is a considerable risk that your investments won't perform as planned and that you will not to be able to afford to retire at the preordained date. Based on current annuity rates, there is also a significant chance that your health may not allow you to work up to the required date, meaning that you may never be in a fit state to enjoy the fruits of your labour when you do retire and start to draw your pension.

Thankfully, there are a great, many alternative approaches available. It really is just a case of expanding your horizons, and adjusting your thinking to operate outside of the system. So now let's look at some real-life case studies of people who have truly retired (in a conventional, end of working life way), but who have done so in a bold and highly unconventional way!

ROCK STAR RETIREMENT– A CASE STUDY

Clive and Jane Green: Around the world in 5,840 days (16 years!) on a shoestring budget

Buying a yacht and sailing around the world sounds like the classic 'rich man's retirement plan.' It also fits into the Rock Star Retirement lifestyle and for your real life rock star role models think Simon and Jasmin Le Bon. However, for most people it remains little more than a vague dream, inspired by a spot of boat watching on an exotic marina during a holiday. For most it falls into the "if I won the lottery" category, with no practical investigation or action ever taken. Yet it really is an option open to almost anyone, if you want it enough and are practical, or prepared to develop the practical skills and commitment to make it happen.

Enter Clive and Jane Green to show how it is done with a truly inspiring story. This is a great tale, but it is not just a story about sailing. It is a superb illustration of a Rock Star Retirement mindset and is something you could apply to any number of different situations. For example, if you get seasick or are not as practical as The Greens then you could easily substitute the boat for a camper van, or motor home, to fulfil your own road trip version of this epic tale.

In 1998 the Greens effectively retired with Clive aged 46 and Jane just 44. They set off from Milford Haven, Wales on July 11, 1998, with the plan of seeing whether they could live comfortably together within the confines of a 35 ft yacht.

They planned a two-week trip that went so well they decided to keep going and in July 2014 *some 16 years later*, they finally returned to their home port to catch up with friends and naturally to think about their next adventure. Here is the staggering itinerary they completed:

1998–1999: After leaving Wales they took in Ireland, Spain, Portugal, Gibraltar, Madeira, Canaries, Cape Verde and Barbados.

2000: St Lucia, St Vincent and the Grenadines, Grenada, Trinidad and Tobago, Venezuela, Martinique, Dominica, Guadeloupe, Antigua and Barbuda.

2001: St Kitts and Nevis, St Maarten, Anguilla, British Virgin Islands, American Virgin Islands, Bermuda, the USA and Canada.

2002–2003: Bahamas, Panama, Galapagos, Marquesas, Tuamotu, Society Islands, Northern Cook Islands, Samoa and Tonga.

2003–2005: New Zealand, Fiji, Vanuatu and New Caledonia.

2005–2007: Australia, Indonesia, Singapore, Malaysia and Thailand.

2009–2011: India, Oman, Yemen, Eritrea, Sudan, Egypt, Cyprus, Turkey, Greece, Bulgaria and Romania.

2012–2014: Greece, Malta, Italy, Spain, Portugal, Azores, Ireland and Wales.

Highlights of their trip included being privileged to see so much of planet earth, unrushed and on their own terms.

"We have been very lucky to see our planet in such an amazing way. We didn't ever plan to sail around the world. It just happened!"

They dodged man-eating komodo dragons, swam with seals, saw glaciers and watched active volcanoes. With no light pollution far out in the oceans, they witnessed amazing starry nights. Along the way, they had encounters with marine iguanas, flying fish, stingrays, turtles and saw whales larger than their own boat.

The kind, generous and inspiring people they met reaffirmed their faith in human nature and that most humans are fundamentally decent people.

On their return, they were amazed by the amount of positive press coverage that their exploits generated. Their story was featured in the major UK newspapers, on national radio and they even made an appearance on breakfast TV.

"We've been completely knocked out by it all", said Jane, 60. "We can't believe it. Why on earth would anyone be interested in us? It's not as if we've really been doing anything."

"And we haven't even had any proper disasters", added Clive, 62. "Disasters sell news, not two people doing a bit of nice sailing."

Somehow this inspired couple have taken the concept of a trip of a lifetime, normally a one-off spectacular two or three week holiday for the average couple and turned it into the trip of a significant part of their lifetimes.

So how did they do it?

They were far from rich in the conventional sense. Still in their 40s, they were a good 20 years younger than the average UK retiree. In fact, when they started off on their sailing odyssey, they were too young to cash in and draw on their pensions. This is a story of desire, initiative and seizing the opportunities that came their way. Clive took voluntary redundancy from his job as an engineer and received a severance package, which allowed him to pay off their mortgage. Jane handed in her notice as a micro-biology technician at a hospital.

Now let's look at some of the numbers. In terms of initial outlay, it cost £16,000 to purchase their boat and a further £21,000 to refit her and bring her up to scratch to make her truly ocean-going.

Adjusted for inflation in today's prices, this would be around £60,000. This is a good sum of money, but probably not as much as you might at first expect. If you are prepared to be frugal and to work really hard for a few years, this is eminently achievable. Full details of exactly how this is possible are available to those who graduate on the full Rock Star Retirement programme.

What about living costs?

For nearly the first decade, until their pensions kicked in, things were tight in terms of their available cash for living expenses. They had spent all of their savings on kitting the boat out and in the early days they had to rely on their own skills to fix problems with the boat. The Greens could not afford to eat out at expensive restaurants.

"It wasn't a holiday, we were on a strict budget so that took some getting used to"

Initially they lived on £130 a week, bartering their few belongings for food and other supplies, including bargaining with one of Jane's bras on an island off Fiji for some fruit.

The £130 a week income came from renting out their house in Wales. They eventually boosted this by selling their family home and buying two smaller properties which provided a higher rental yield. In later years this was further supplemented as their pensions kicked in.

The Greens' big adventure teaches us a number of highly valuable lessons.

★ You don't have to wait until you are in your 60s. Retirement can be, to some extent, a lifestyle choice. Based on normal life expectancy (currently 81.5 years in the UK) Clive and Jane are likely to spend around half of their lives 'retired,' doing what they want to do.

★ You don't need to be rich to live a life less ordinary.

★ There really is nothing to stop you living your own Rock Star Retirement, you just need to follow the lead from those who have been successful and make your own plan.

★ For couples, shared interests and a shared goal are the key to happiness. This would not have worked if one of the couple did not like sailing. The Greens were already keen sailors, so it was not a pipe dream. This was their second boat and they had hands-on experience of refurbishing boats and all aspects of sailing to give them the confidence, developed over a 10-year period before their round the world odyssey.

★ Clive seized the opportunity of voluntary redundancy which provided a lump sum to facilitate some of the financial aspects at such a relatively young age. Although you may not be lucky enough to be offered a pay off by your employer, it is possible to reduce debt or build up savings relatively quickly, but it takes sacrifice and discipline.

★ The Greens had no children or dependants, so they were relatively free to just cut anchor and sail away. However, if you do have children, there are ways to accommodate them via home schooling while giving them an amazing education on the seven seas!

Too radical?

While I personally love adventure and travel, we are all different and I do appreciate that many people are home birds. For those who suffer from seasickness and for those based in land-locked locations, this sailing dream is a non-starter! If the thought of leaving your country of birth is a nightmare for you then I respect this. However, if this is the case then it is important to be grateful for the country you reside in and to appreciate what you have. Moaning about your life but doing nothing to change it is NOT a Rock Star Retiree characteristic. If whinging about your country is one of your behaviours, then spending time overseas, even for a short holiday, is a great way to gain a true perspective of what you actually have in your home country, or whether there are better options available. However, beware! A two-week luxury holiday in the sun can provide a distorted view of another country. You need to be realistic and to spend some proper time researching the reality of day-to-day life and culture in that country.

Like the Greens, the protagonists of our next case study made some bold decisions and opted for an equally unorthodox approach to retirement. However, in this case, they had children and grandchildren and so elected to stay a little closer to home.

ROCK STAR RETIREMENT – CASE STUDY

Bruce and Sheila Napier: Creating a life with 'sanity again'

In the UK there are over 3,000 miles of navigable inland waterways with rivers and canals hosting 88,000 registered boats. Many are small pleasure cruisers moored close to their owners' homes, effectively holiday homes on the water used for getaways at weekends and on long summer evenings. However, an estimated 22,000 are 'liveaboards', boats used as permanent homes on the water.

Great Britain was the cradle of the industrial revolution and possesses the most densely concentrated network of canals, however, there are also many more thousands of miles of rivers and navigable inland waterways in central Europe, North America and beyond. Thanks to the historic Magna Carta of 1215, there are even moorings in prime spots in some of the most exclusive areas of London. For those who don't have the sailing experience, or the sea legs for the Greens' epic ocean-conquering odyssey cited in case study 2, inland waterways provide a more sedate, and readily accessible, alternative lifestyle choice.

The first case study interview conducted for this book took place in the autumn of 2014. To assist with my research, the UK Canal and River Trust had kindly arranged for me to meet Bruce and Sheila Napier to talk about their experiences of retiring early and living the last decade aboard their own purpose-built narrow barge called Sanity Again.

Having arrived early, I was able to enjoy a coffee on the wooden decking area of their local cafe at the marina in Derbyshire where the Napiers' narrowboat is moored, the place they call home when they are not "cruising." It was a glorious morning, the sky a deep indigo and the country air so crisp and fresh that it made the very act of breathing feel like an indulgent pleasure. The leaves on the oak and beech trees were at the crescendo of their autumnal palette, a riot of ochre and copper, while the willow trees at the water's edge provided rich, defiant contrast as they held on to their lush green foliage, despite the changing of the seasons. It was one of those rare Indian summer mornings, a day that lifts your spirits and demands that you remember that right here, right now is a great place to be, a great moment to be alive. A pair of mute swans promenaded their young family back and forth, adding dynamism to the scene and for a few precious minutes I completely lost myself in the beauty of the moment, completely forgetting the bigger picture of why I was there. For me it was a timely reminder: focus on big goals and ideas, but enjoy the small stuff too.

The Napiers' story

The Napiers joined me for a drink. Warm and open, they were an instantly likeable couple. Bruce the more chatty, Sheila more economic with her words, but insightful with her contributions. They both exuded an air of wisdom born of the luxury of time to think, time to put their universe into order and from contentment with their lot in life.

In my experience of selling small businesses, there is generally a long drawn-out thought process preceding the sale. Most people fear change and have a tendency to procrastinate rather than risk uncertainty. Sometimes owners can think about selling their business for many years. For action to occur, there almost always needs to be a trigger to motivate the person enough to finally act decisively. The death, or illness, of a close friend or relative of a similar age can wake a person up to their own mortality and the uncertain nature of their health as they get older. Triggers also can be positive too, a financial windfall can change the stakes, or the jealousy/desire to join a close friend or relative who is happily retired and enjoying life on the golf course also feature highly. The same principal appears to apply to the Rock Star Retirement concept too. If we go back to the Greens in case study 2, it was when Clive was offered voluntary redundancy with a generous severance package that catalysed the Greens to up sticks and sail off round the world for almost two decades.

For the Napiers, the catalyst was the death of one of Bruce's colleagues almost immediately after he retired at the age of just 60. This event appears to have crystallised their thinking and as a consequence, the Napiers do not consider their early retirement lifestyle choice to be unorthodox. For them, it was a very logical decision to quit the rat race and live a simpler, less consumer oriented lifestyle doing what they loved, boating.

Sheila summed up the thought process behind their move beautifully: *"We had a choice. We could wait another 10 years for the safety net of a big pension, but risk uncertainty over our future health and ability to enjoy life, or we could seize the day and live our love of boating on a tighter budget. For us it was a no-brainer."*

So how did they do it?

Once the decision had been made, they effectively liquidated their assets by selling off their family home, the bulk of their possessions and when everything was in place, even their cars. There was to be no going back! The proceeds of the sale of their home in Anglesey and most of their possessions, enabled them to buy their own boat, Sanity and to invest the remaining capital to provide a subsistence income. At the ages of 54 and 55, they had successfully quit the rat race and joined the Rock Star Retirees, living life on their own terms.

With our drinks finished, the Napiers kindly invited me to visit their home to give me a better feel for how they lived. Their boat's name, Sanity Again, is a playful nod to Bruce's former career as a psychologist.[32] It also aptly describes the life it has given them away from the pressures of work and conventional living. I would describe life aboard as comfortable and cosy, rather than luxurious.

The rocking motion onboard was much greater than I would have expected for a berthed boat in a calm marina, but I am sure you get used to this pretty quickly. According to the Napiers, much of the appeal of inland boating comes from being outside and enjoying the moving landscape and the connection with nature and other boaters.

It is blissful in the warmer months, but tougher during the winter. However, Mercia Marina, where their boat now resides when they are not cruising is not just a pretty backdrop. It boasts substantial facilities to make the colder winter months onboard much more agreeable. In addition to the excellent cafe where we met, the marina houses a traditional butchers shop, an upmarket bistro, a chandlers/hardware store and a high-end farm shop.

The crowning glory for me though is the mobile fish and chip van which visits every Friday evening to feed the hungry boaters, now that is what I call living! For the water dwelling residents, the marina is a perfect blend of bohemian living supplemented with all the mod cons, including Wi-Fi.

However, the Napiers' boat has not always been moored in such luxurious surroundings. Indeed in the early days money was extremely tight. Until their pensions kicked in the Napiers lived on a budget of just £12,000 a year. Bruce explained to me that on the

---

[32] Their first boat was named "Sanity"

UK's inland waterways, it is mandatory to register boats as either pleasure boats or liveaboards. Boats registered as liveaboards are categorised as permanent dwellings and as such have to be declared as a home, or permanent mooring. This costs around £3,000 per annum and on an extremely tight budget in the early years was not a viable option for the Napiers. Instead, for the first six years of living on the UK's canals, Bruce and Sheila elected for a semi-nomadic existence of 'continuous cruising.' This meant that they were not legally able to moor in the same place for more than 14 days.

Later on, their pensions provided additional income and eased the pressure a little. More recently, Sheila received some inheritance from an aunt which they invested in a log cabin on the marina. It serves as both an investment vehicle to provide annual income and a holiday home for their children and grandchildren.

The highlights of the Napiers' ongoing adventures are numerous and are now well documented. Bruce started a daily blog to keep their children and grandchildren in touch with their adventures. This project expanded into a winter project which turned into a book, "Building Sanity Again". Sheila quickly got in on the act with "Tales from the Towpath" and "A Boater's Commonplace Book " before Bruce completed "Practically Cooking on Board".

The books are now sold as e-books providing a small additional income for the Napiers, but also some genuine rivalry as to who has sold the most! For anyone seriously contemplating buying, building or living on a narrow boat, these are invaluable resources, they are also a great read. However, for a real-life day-to-day balanced view on boating, Bruce's blog is the place for me. It is an honest and representative account of the joys and trials of daily living, from baking fresh bread onboard, to the nuances of the different types of rain that afflict the UK boater. All written from the perspective of a happy couple living life on their own terms.

CANAL ROCK STAR
REFERENCE

In the summer of 2004, Hollywood A-Lister Harrison Ford and his wife Calista Flockhart (better known as Ali McBeal) were spotted enjoying a narrowboat holiday in Shropshire on the Llangollen Canal. In an interview for the Sunday Times, the star of Indiana Jones and Star Wars said:

"It was just the four of us, me, Calista, Liam and the nanny. I found it relaxing and fun and the rest of the family loved it. You can see the English countryside in a way you can't when you're speeding down the M1!"

Okay, so Harrison is a film star, rather than a rock star, but back in 2004 Harrison and Calista made narrowboating sexy so I had to put it in!

LESSON 2 SUMMARY

Our life plan is mapped out from an early age. It involves choosing a career and then investing time in developing specialist skills and experience in the chosen field in return for a reward package.

Across a diverse range of sectors, people often find that the day-to-day experience of doing the job is very different from what they had expected. However, having invested a number of years acquiring niche skills and experience, they often feel committed and trapped. Changing careers and learning new skills is likely to involve a significant reduction in earning power for a number of years until they have mastered the new field. With financial and family commitments, many people feel forced to grin and bear their deeply unsatisfactory jobs, even though they spend more of their waking hours at work than anywhere else.

Once 'trapped,' these people begin to resent their jobs and in order to get by, fixate upon their retirement which they perceive as their only means of escaping the day-to-day drudgery of their jobs.

We recapped on the fact that based on the huge number of variables, both financial and health wise this is a very risky strategy. There is a very real danger that this golden retirement is never realised at all.

Lesson 2 then provided a number of case studies illustrating different escape strategies utilised by real life people who found themselves in this predicament:

The first case study recounted how Lindsey, a primary school teacher transferred her existing skills from the UK to Melbourne. In Australia, she successfully secured a job with a smaller class size, and a more positive working culture that allowed her to minimise administration and focus on teaching — a job that she absolutely loved and that actually paid her more.

The second case study illustrated John's story, involving a bold and dramatic change of career, from an executive to a self-employed chimney sweep. Based on every metric that matters, this proved to be an inspired decision for John.

We then moved onto the first of our 'permanent' retirement case studies. Examples of people who retired completely from their working lives in the conventional sense, but who facilitated their retirements in highly unconventional ways, enabling them to follow their dreams at a much younger age, to avoid them gambling with the time/money/health conundrum.

This brings us nicely onto the next lesson: **Rockstar health**

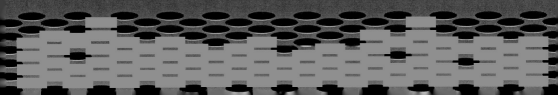

LESSON 3

ROCK STAR HEALTH

LOOKING AFTER THE VESSEL YOU SAIL IN

He said, "Call the doctor. I think I'm gonna crash."

"The doctor say he's coming but you gotta pay in cash."
They were rushing down that freeway, messed around and
got lost. They didn't care they were just dyin' to get off.

And it was life in the fast lane ....

EAGLES — Life In The Fast Lane

And now for something completely different

What is the first image that comes into your mind when you think about the combination of "Rock Star" and "health?" It is safe to say that it is unlikely to be a pretty picture. The lives of real life rock stars are synonymous with sex, drugs and rock 'n' roll with the rock star ranks littered with the victims of famously excessive lifestyles and the tragic, untimely end of talented artists.

During the research for this book, I was surprised by the sheer scale of untimely deaths. Have you heard of the infamous 27 Club, a celebrated group of musicians who all departed from this mortal coil at the age of just 27? The most famous members are:

★ Brian Jones (original member of the Rolling Stones) who drowned in a swimming pool, thought to be drug related.

★ Jimi Hendrix who died of a combination of drugs/alcohol/asphyxiation

★ Janis Joplin who had a drug overdose

★ Jim Morrison another drug overdose*

★ Kurt Cobain who committed suicide

★ Amy Winehouse whose death was due to a combination of drugs and alcohol on a body greatly weakened by bulimia.

Not pretty reading is it. And outside of this unfortunate club, there are scores more of different ages, such as Buddy Holly who died at the tender age of 21 through to Michael Hutchence of the band INXS, who at 37 died just before he had a chance to contemplate middle age. Arguably the most infamous premature and undignified death of them all was Elvis Presley. The King of Rock and Roll died rather unglamorously on his 'throne' (the toilet) at the age of 42, an obese insomniac whose addiction to prescription drugs resulted in a massively enlarged liver, chronic constipation and a fatal heart attack.

This group of legendary musicians and their movie star cousins (James Dean, Marilyn Munroe, River Phoenix) somehow in death become mythical figures. While it is a slightly morose subject, for many people it also carries a guilty fascination. This can be seen by the fact that in death, many artists end up selling significantly more music, films and merchandise and having far more books written about them than when they were alive. It is an interesting subject, but I think it is safe to say that none of these represent the kind of Rock Star Retirement or health plan that you or I are aspiring to! So what can we learn from these short-lived legends without becoming too morbid or getting into conspiracy theories about the real causes of their early demise?

ROCK STAR RETIREMENT TIP:

*if your band is no longer making sweet music,
before you hang up your guitar, maybe it's time to go solo,
get a new producer or try a different record label!*

*There is almost certainly another great performance
in you yet.*

Lessons from a Rock Star genie

Rock Star warning: I have to confess to having a bit of fun creating the next section and while no illicit substances were taken during the writing, from a Rock Star perspective, this was definitely my experimental, psychedelic writing phase! (All good aspiring Rock artists and Rock Star Retirees have them as part of their journey.) Despite the playful nature, there is an important underlying message that should not be overlooked.

Suppose you found a magic electric guitar, a very special instrument that when strummed, summoned a rock and roll genie. Today you would probably stumble upon this brilliant find via an eBay auction or perhaps Alibaba.com rather than a secret cave. Whatever the case — cave with a magic door, or a password-protected website — if you are anything like me, then the struggle to 'recall' the code to grant entry would have proven equally challenging. However, I digress, how you came across the genie is not important, it is what the genie can do that is of interest — and how you choose to use it.

With the guitar strummed and the genie deployed from the **magic amp** (oh come on, it was too good to leave out) it is time to make your wishes. But this is no ordinary genie, this is a Rock Star genie and the wishes he can grant, although still pretty cool, are very specific.

In truth, he is a bit of a one trick pony (some might argue a bit like Status Quo whose songs all seem to be written using exactly the same three chords. *RIP Rick*) In fact the genie can really only grant you one wish but you get to make the wish three times! Confused? Let me explain the scenario.

You are going to enjoy a legendary night out in the VIP area of the world's coolest club. It is in a secret location in Paris and as you would expect, entry is by invitation only. For your special night, the drinks are on the house, which is a very good thing because you would not believe the prices. Think that you are too old to enjoy clubbing? Don't worry, I promise you there will be some other veterans joining you to make you feel right at home.

Viewed from the outside there is nothing ostentatious about the club building. However, once you enter and walk down the flight of 27 worn, red carpeted steps and turn a corner, I guarantee that, you will never have seen anything like it. The high ceilinged interior is both expansive and intimate, a juxtaposition achieved by stunning design, using every trick in the book: warm accent walls and clever placement of soft furnishings and objects d'art all showcased by state-of-the-art dynamic mood lighting and a 4D sound system. The walls and interior spaces are adorned with Damian Hirst sculptures, Banksy artwork and priceless rock star memorabilia.

When you are shown to the VIP area, you will find one of Jimmy Hendrix's guitars, framed original handwritten John Lennon lyrics, and, of course, one of Madonna's corsets.[33]

There are also ice sculptures, a Champagne fountain, a hot tub and live music from some of the world's top acts in the most intimate of settings.[34] When you feel peckish, there is a top Parisian chef on call to make whatever you fancy. However, be warned, whether it's a humble cheese toastie, or something more highbrow, like lobster thermidor for example, he will find a way to incorporate his signature combination of gold leaf and truffles into the dish in some way.

All pretty amazing, definitely a unique 'money can't buy experience,' but nothing magical yet. So now that the scene is set, let's get back to the genie, the magic amp and those outstanding wishes. It is time for a Ringo Starr drumroll to accompany the big reveal. The genie's special power relates to your choice of company for this amazing night out. Each of your wishes is a choice of a genuine Rock Star companion to join you in the VIP lounge. However, as I pre-warned you, this is no ordinary genie and these wishes are pretty extraordinary too, or to be more precise **paranormal.** You see, you don't get to choose from the ranks of living artists — your options are limited to an even more exclusive, select group, the ghosts of Rock Stars prematurely past. This is going to be some night out!

Exercise:

Which three **permanently** retired (AKA prematurely deceased) rock stars would you choose to share your magical night out with?

---

[33] The poor woman seems to leave her underwear all over the show, but this particular exhibit is a bit special, it is encrusted with gemstones and was made for the launch of her film Truth or Dare at the 1990 Cannes film festival

[34] I know I instructed you to throw them away several times, but rocking a pair of real rose tinted spectacles/shades would seriously go down a storm in this place

HINT: The most popular candidates for this exercise are: John Lennon, David Bowie, Freddie Mercury, Prince, Elvis and Buddy Holly. However, the prematurely deceased rock star graveyard is your oyster! If you are struggling, then it might be helpful to look back at the earlier part of this lesson for inspiration on some of the options. The 27 club has some intriguing characters. When you have made your choices, please write in your answers below:

Premature Rock Star ghost choice

1: _____

2: _____

3: _____

Your choice of Rock Star companions will vary depending upon your age, musical taste and other individual preferences. There are no right or wrong answers — whatever floats your boat! You may be wondering what the relevance of this is and where exactly are we going with it? Now here is the thing. It goes without saying that you would have an amazing night out sharing this exclusive Parisian club setting with three top legends. Indeed, I suspect it might well involve a world class karaoke session and that you are guaranteed to come away with some killer selfies with your idols. Yet what I think would be really interesting are the reflections and insights that these real life, prematurely retired Rock Stars could tell us from the 'other side'. To illustrate this, and to have a bit more fun, here is my own list and what I think these superstars might want to share with us:

Rock Star: Michael Hutchence, lead singer of INXS

Revelation 1: "Money and fame can become a trap, they are both addictive and destructive. What made me truly happy was a handful of loving close relationships. Be careful what you wish for"

Revelation 2: "INXS's music still sounds great today, I am immensely proud of my musical legacy and for putting Australia on the world music map"

 Rock Star: Elvis Presley

Revelation 1: "I had so much money, fame and world-wide adoration, yet what really made me happy was escaping from being Elvis and simply being a father to Lisa Marie"

Revelation 2: "Well bless my soul what's wrong with me, truffle on a cheeseburger who'd ever believe, can I order another one pronto please, Mm mm oh, yeah, I'm all shook up!" Well what did you expect? This is supposed to be a great night out, not just a philosophy lesson! Personally, I was just pleased that he had got his appetite back.

 Rock Star: Marilyn Monroe[35]

Revelation 1: As I have explained at some length to my long suffering wife, my interest in meeting Marilyn Monroe would be purely for research purposes. Although I have to admit that this timeless movie star would add a bit of feminine sassiness and fun to the evening "Yes, I can confirm that I had an affair with President JFK.....but there was no conspiracy and nothing sinister in my death. I took my own life ....why? My entire, career and sense of self-worth were based on my

---

[35] Not technically a rock star (although she did a fair bit of singing) but as you will see throughout the book, my definition of rock star has been expanded to include shining lights from all fields, from authors, to businessmen to actors and, of course, non-famous people who simply take control of their own lives and destinies to make the most of them to become Rock Star Retirees.

looks. At the age of 36, I was struggling with the physical ageing process and with what the future had in store for me. 1950s Hollywood was not a forgiving place for an ageing female movie star

Revelation 2: "While Hollywood is the ultimate bubble, we all exist in a very small part of the real world. We **all** live in a bubble. At times it becomes difficult to see what is important and what is real as opposed to what we think is important and what we think is real

Author's admission of a guilty pleasure — beauty and wisdom, what a woman!

Key Takeaways:

These departed stars were celebrated, rich and highly successful within their own short lifetimes. To some extent, they had all fulfilled their goals, dreams and desires. Yet they were deeply unhappy and this then manifested itself in coping strategies, escape tactics and habits that ultimately proved terminally destructive on their physical health. While they are extreme examples, the same principals apply to everyone.

Think **deeply** about what you really want and what truly makes you happy. Being a member of Guns N' Roses is not necessarily always going to be a bed of roses. Retiring from your work at an unorthodoxly young age and spending your time lying on a beach, or shopping 'til you drop each day may superficially sound attractive to some people, but it is highly unlikely to prove to be your Nirvana. In other words, you need to make sure that you are not escaping from one unsatisfactory reality to replace it with another one.

Success comes at a price. While on one hand, the relentless pursuit and mastery of big goals is admirable, to achieve any goal carries a price. In the same way that there is a risk of dying before you reach retirement via the conventional financial advisers recommended route, there is also a risk that you achieve your goal, but that the pace and intensity you set yourself, ultimately destroys your ability to enjoy the fruits of your victory. The timeless rock star example of this is the founding story of the marathon. Here is Runner's World account of this epically tragic event:

"After the badly outnumbered Greeks somehow managed to drive back the Persians who had invaded the coastal plain of Marathon, an Athenian messenger named Pheidippides was dispatched from the battlefield to Athens to deliver the news of Greek victory. After running about 25 miles to the Acropolis, he burst into the chambers and gallantly hailed his countrymen with "Nike! Nike! Nenikekiam" ("Victory! Victory! Rejoice, we conquer!"). And then he promptly collapsed from exhaustion and died."

This is not as abstract as it first might seem. I have had to sell plenty of businesses over the years because the owners have had such an intensity of focus that they have neglected everything else, including their health. As a result, some have quite literally driven themselves into an early grave, others have become incapacitated by a stroke or heart attack rendering them unable to enjoy the financial success their businesses have become.

My Rock Star Retirement mentors are unanimous in the fact that when it comes to big, life-defining goals, it is essential to make sure that **your chosen destination is genuinely worth dying for and the journey to achieving it is worth living for.**

Take a minute to re-read this last sentence and to reflect on its meaning. Now review your own Rock Star Retirement goals. If they don't pass this acid test then it is time to go back to the drawing board.

In terms of health, the brain and the body work in tandem. To maintain peak physical fitness, you need to have good mental health first. Coming to terms with ageing can be challenging, unless you have the right mental strategies. We will cover these in a separate lesson later — the Rock Star Mindset.

So far I have only mentioned examples of real life rock stars who met with tragic ends. Are there any "healthy" rock stars who can point the way for us?

Thankfully there are some rock stars that have managed to buck the self-destruct trend. Some are reformed bad boys, or drug addicts, and there are even a select few who have managed to avoid the excesses of the rock and roll lifestyle altogether.

The top five healthy rock star hit parade

At number 5, we have the Red Hot Chilli Peppers' lead singer Anthony Kiedis. Now well into his 50s, this middle age-defying rock god has the face and body of a 30-year-old. He has become the model for Rock Star healthy living, but it has not always been this way! He put his Dorian Gray-like attributes down to discovering surfing later in life to keep his mind and body young, leading to a raft of other health-reinforcing habits.

A new entry at number four, is former Police frontman and a very reformed Sting: "I spent most of my life looking for the quick fix and the deep kick. I shot drugs under freeway off-ramps with Mexican gang-bangers and in $1,000 a day hotel suites. Now I sip vitamin-infused water and seek out wild, as opposed to farm-raised salmon." *Can you believe that he is now in his 60s?*

Remaining at number three, we have the material girl herself, the queen of pop, Madonna. Despite some headline-grabbing bedroom habits, she adheres to a rigorous diet and fitness regime to stave off the aging process. Aside from the odd slip down a staircase, this lady can still seriously dance.[36]

Close, but no cigar (he is in the healthy Rock Star top five after all) it's Bruce Springsteen, perhaps exceptional because he is reported by his bandmates never to have touched drugs. Now in his mid-60s, he is still the same weight as when he was 15. For the last 30+ years he has adhered to a fitness regime of running on a treadmill and lifting weights, a mostly vegetarian diet, relaxing with his family and reading books.

---

[36]   And rapidly approaching her 70s, this apparently highly sexed woman certainly supports my assertion in Lesson 1 that peoples sex lives are likely to continue into their 70s and 80s!

At number one we have the Rock Health King, Mick Jagger. While some might claim that his amazing vitality is because he is pickled and smoked, this dinosaur Rock God has surprisingly hidden depths and a killer health regime.[37] A graduate of the London School of Economics in 1963, it has been calculated that at an average Rolling Stones concert during his highly active performances, he covers 12 miles (we are talking about massive stadiums with runways out into the crowd).

Key Take Aways

The main takeaway message from the select bunch of thriving rock legends is that it is possible to turn things around. Rock stars and 'real people' can successfully turn around a toxic, destructive lifestyle and move on to thrive. If you currently smoke, are overweight or have other self-inflicted issues, it is possible to turn your ship around.

[37]   And in 2017 at the age of 73, he became a father again, proving that his health regime is clearly working in all areas

LESSON 3 SUMMARY

The realm of the real life Rock Star is a place of excess and fast living. Rock stars and their celebrated movie star cousins are synonymous with poor health habits and (as the 27 Club starkly reminds us) a very short life-span.

A life dependent on rehab and shrinks, or a life cut dramatically short is certainly not the kind of Rock Star Retirement that we are aspiring to here!

We did not delve into this area purely out of morbid curiosity. There are important lessons that can be gleaned to help guide us to better form and plan our own aspirations and goals.

The Rock Star Genie exercise highlighted that most of these early departed Rock Stars had achieved their goals and dreams of wealth, success and fame. Despite this they were unhappy and unfulfilled.

Achieving celebrity status and critical acclaim does not automatically lead to happiness for real Rock Stars. In the same vein your dream of an ideal life and retirement if not fully thought through, may not make you happy either. Spending a lifetime of sacrifice working to reach nirvana and then finding out it is actually not the Promised Land at all can be a shattering blow—and like with real Rock Stars, it can lead to depression and ill health.

On the other hand, taking a different path and shooting for unusual or exceptional things with your life carries risks too. For those with big goals and aspirations, be prepared to make the necessary sacrifices.

When it comes to Rock Star health, not all of the outcomes are bad. Some exceptions like Bruce Springsteen managed to remain physically and mentally well despite the distractions of success, wealth and fame. More significantly, there are plenty of examples of Rock Stars who managed to clean up and turn around unhealthy or even toxic lifestyles and to transform themselves into paragons of health.

Staying in good health in our later years does not happen by accident, it is something that has to be actively worked at via a disciplined regime of healthy eating and exercise.

There is no point in planning and working towards your own version of a Rock Star retirement, if you don't look after yourself along the way. You may not be in any fit state to enjoy it when you get there, if you make it at all, and if you are healthy and approach things in the right way, the journey can be as fun as the destination.

Look after the vessel you sail in.

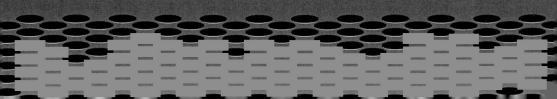

LESSON 4

DRUGS AND ROCK AND ROLL

One pill makes you larger, and one pill makes you small
And the ones that mother gives you, don't do anything at all
Go ask Alice, when she's ten feet tall

And if you go chasing rabbits,
and you know you're going to fall
Tell 'em a hookah-smoking caterpillar has
given you the call
And call Alice, when she was just small

When the men on the chessboard get up and tell
you where to go
And you've just had some kind of mushroom,
and your mind is moving low
Go ask Alice, I think she'll know

When logic and proportion have fallen sloppy dead
And the white knight is talking backwards
And the red queen's off with her head
Remember what the dormouse said
Feed your head, feed your head

GRACE SLICK — *White Rabbit*

DRUGS AND ROCK
AND ROLL

Ok, now we are talking! When it comes to the lives of real rock stars, drugs are never too far away. But the drugs you need to proactively understand and harness, to help you achieve your Rock Star Retirement are very different from the CLASS A drugs that would inevitably lead you to rehab, or even worse, the 27 club.

We are, of course, talking about natural drugs. Organic chemicals found in the food and drink we consume and perhaps less well understood, mood altering drugs produced by our own bodies, in the amazing mini pharmaceutical factory located at the base of our brainstem and elsewhere.

The most important drugs are a quartet of naturally occurring 'drugs' responsible for our motivation, happiness and ability to focus. The first two, endorphins and dopamine are fairly well-known, the remaining two, serotonin and oxytocin may be less familiar, but all are important to help keep us feeling happy, fulfilled and in balance.

Whilst Dr Watson[38] has a certain ring to it ("elementary my Dear Watson"), I am neither a doctor nor a scientist. My understanding of this cocktail of wellbeing chemicals is therefore based on more eminent and suitably qualified people's research. Having read up on the science and applied it to practical strategies and an overall methodology for utilising the knowledge to promote a more positive approach to life, I can say with certitude that the science does hold up to scrutiny – although it is

---

[38] If there are any university deans reading this from any of the four universities I attended, or indeed any other benevolent academic institutions, then I am all ears if you would like to offer me an honorary doctorate (Go on, you would be helping me tick another item off my bucket list. Let me explain my affliction! Whenever I have to give my surname, checking in at hotels, airports etc, I am pretty much always asked (in an ironic kind of a way) "you are not Doctor Watson are you?" After years of this well-meaning torture, it would feel so nice to be able to say yes!)

admittedly difficult to isolate any single chemical and its effect in isolation. Let's take a quick look at the science.

Chemical: Dopamine

Function: Dopamine is a natural drug that is believed to provide us with the motivation to take action toward goals, desires and needs. Neuroscientists sometimes refer to it as the "reward molecule". It provides us with a biochemically induced surge of satisfaction when we achieve a goal.

Have you ever found yourself writing items onto your 'to do' list that you have already completed, just so that you can enjoy the satisfaction of ticking them off or crossing them out? This is a classic example of the power of dopamine and is a surprisingly common behaviour, induced by the fact that we receive a little dose from the action of crossing something off our lists.

On the flip side of the equation, self-doubt and procrastination are linked with low levels of dopamine.

It is thought that some highly successful people may have naturally occurring higher levels of dopamine that helps them to stay "on task" longer and therefore to achieve more. However, there is arguably a degree of chicken and egg syndrome going on here. Without a realistic vision or plan to provide achievable objectives, dopamine production is likely to diminish, so this is in most cases a self-fulfilling feedback loop.

Ways to boost and use to improve our lives: A starting point is to produce a list of written goals to aim for. Get excited by the thought of how achieving these goals will make you feel – optimism generates dopamine.

Break the big goals down into smaller sub-tasks [sometimes referred to as chunking.]

Rather than restricting celebrations to when we hit the big goal finish line, this approach means that we can create a series of smaller 'milestone' achievements, to tick off.

Each little victory, takes us a step closer towards the big picture goal, triggering a self-reinforcing release of dopamine to help us on our way.

Use the discipline and techniques available on the online Rock Star Retirement programme to make sure that you are on the right side of the feedback-loop equation.

Chemical: Endorphins

Endorphins are most famously known for providing 'runners high' after a vigorous run or exercise session, often articulated as a feeling of 'euphoria.' Endorphins are actually released in response to pain and stress, acting in a similar way to morphine, by reducing our perception of pain. They have also been found to alleviate anxiety and depression. So a small amount of stress in our lives in certain forms is not necessarily a bad thing. However, at the other end of the spectrum, like any other drug, endorphins can become highly addictive.

Real life rock star example of how NOT to do it!

"I became a hamster, 17 miles a day on a treadmill!" American rapper Eminem famously swapped a drug addiction for a running addiction.

Ways to boost and use to improve our lives: Exercise is the most obvious way to promote the endorphin feel-good factor. This is why I and countless others lace up our trainers whenever we have had a bad day.

If you are not into running, there are other ways to get your fix.

★ Laughter offers a less physically exertive way to induce endorphin release.

★ Various studies have claimed that the smell of vanilla and also lavender can stimulate endorphin production (aromatherapy), as well as spicy food and dark chocolate.

I am not 100% convinced by these claims. For example, if you have a curry and then have to run to the toilet, the key question for me is whether the endorphins are produced because of the curry or the run to the bathroom!

Chemical: Serotonin

Serotonin is secreted [mainly in your gut] when you feel 'worthy' or important and when in turn your life feels meaningful.

An absence of serotonin is associated with loneliness and depression.

The vast majority of anti-depressant medications are focused on stimulating/boosting the production of serotonin.

Brings a whole new perspective to the concept of a 'gut feeling'.

Ways to boost and use to improve our lives: Have you ever woken up in the middle of the night after a nightmare and found yourself really stressed and unable to get back to sleep? During your bad dream, your brain secreted adrenalin as part of your normal fight or flight reflex response to stress and it takes a while for this to wear off. This is because the human brain has trouble telling the difference between what is real and imagined. Knowing this provides us with strategies for stimulating serotonin.

Remember lesson one, where we took the time to get a context on our lives and the opportunities afforded to us compared to our forefathers? Being grateful for what we have (gratitude practice) can help us feel meaningful and can help us produce serotonin.

Reflecting on past achievements allows us to relive the experience. As can having a plan and visualising/fantasising about the outcomes – for example imagining the satisfaction you will enjoy when you get your first book published, have a meal on the Sydney harbour front or running that first 5k without walking.

Vitamin D sourced in humans via exposure to sunlight also promotes serotonin production. Making sure that you receive 20 minutes of natural daylight each day can help with this [not always possible in my home town Manchester!]

Chemical: Oxytocin

Oxytocin is believed to be essential for healthy relationships by creating intimacy and trust. A good example of how this works is that when the release of oxytocin is suppressed in animals, this is when they will reject their offspring.

It is not very rock and roll, but oxytocin increases fidelity. It is essential for creating strong interpersonal bonds and improved social interactions. In humans, the role of oxytocin is not limited to intimate family relationships. It is also essential for building 'bonds' in other relationships too, helping to create friendships and team spirit among colleagues and collaborators, within your own tribes.

Ways to boost and use to improve our lives: Sometimes described as the 'cuddle hormone', an easy way to stimulate the production of oxytocin is to give someone a hug! When someone receives a gift, their oxytocin levels can rise. You can strengthen personal and also work relationships through a simple birthday or anniversary gift.

The odd random act of kindness to someone you know, whether it is a family member, a neighbour or a colleague will make you both feel good and will help to grow a closer, deeper relationship.

Rock Star Retiree Rehab

Experimenting with drugs is an integral part of the Rock Star journey, but for those on the Rock Star Retirement path, the pharmaceuticals of choice are a very different class of drug.

Having taken the time to obtain a basic understanding of these natural, mood enhancing drugs, there is now a huge reward available to you.

The key take away is that there are numerous activities and behaviours that can be adopted to boost your internal production of these 'positivity boosters.'

If you are feeling down, unfulfilled, or under-appreciated, then there is an activity that you can do to start to address this and improve your mood right away – both in the short and the long-term.

What's more, frequently, the human body cannot distinguish between a real event and the mind thinking deeply about an event, or action and how it will feel.

This means that in many cases, simply by starting to think positively about the remedy and by visualising and planning how you can utilise this knowledge, it will actually stimulate production of some of these feel good pharmaceuticals as though the event has taken place. These are powerful drugs and this is powerful medicine indeed.

Make sure you utilise this knowledge consistently to enhance your life every single day.

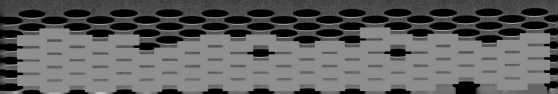

LESSON 5

ROCK STAR AGEING

"I used to jog,
but the ice cubes kept falling
out of my glass"

DAVE LEE ROTH OF VAN HALEN, 1979

SO WHAT EXACTLY IS
AGEING?

The Oxford English Dictionary describes ageing as *"the process of growing old."* However, the biological explanation is much more useful. Contrary to what most people think, ageing is not the accumulation of wear and tear on the body. After all, how much of your body is actually your 'original' body?

Why your body is like a broom

Consider the life of a sweeping brush. (A broom that is lucky enough to reside in a socially responsible and environmentally friendly household that believes in re-use and recycling!) As the bristles wear out with use, the broom head gets replaced. Then inevitably after a few broom heads have come and gone, the handle begins to wear out and this in turn is replaced. After a few years of use, the thrifty owner ends up with a broom that is totally comprised of new parts.

The human body deals with wear and tear mostly in the same way. With a few exceptions such as your teeth, the cells of your body are constantly dying and being regenerated and replaced. And, as with the different parts of the broom, different types of cells have differing lifespans:

★ Oxygen-carrying red blood cells live for about four months.

★ White blood cells — the champions of your body's defence system — live for around a year.

★ Skin cells live for around a fortnight.

★ Sperm cells exist for around four days.

★ Rather poetically, your colon cells get the 'bum' end of the deal and are replaced around every three days!

★ Brain cells are a special case and we will come to these later[39].

★ The biological explanation for ageing comes from the fact that each time a cell is regenerated, a slightly imperfect copy is made and it deteriorates a little.[40] Massive leaps are being made into understanding this cell ageing process which will no doubt lead to significant breakthroughs.[41] However, at this point in time, I am sad to report that physical ageing is inevitable. It cannot yet be reversed and it cannot be 'cured' — fact. There is no point bemoaning it or losing sleep over it (indeed as we will see in a minute, this would be counter-productive).

It is not an even playing field either. Some people naturally age at different rates from others for instance, I started to get the first signs of grey hair at the age of 17!

No matter how healthy your lifestyle is, as your cells regenerate, over time your body will change. While there are some things we can do to slow the process, ageing is 100% inevitable. The only option you have in your control is how you are going to deal with it. Waste your life worrying about it, or face it and embrace it?

It's a dog's life: A Context on The Speed of Ageing:

Consider the life expectancy of man's best friend. Dogs appear to be one of the happiest species on the planet. They run around, play and eat at 100mph, love and sleep deeply, seemingly without a care in the world (have you ever heard of an anorexic dog?) Yet depending upon the breed, dogs typically live for between 10–13 years. Not long is it? However, they don't dwell on it, they don't sweat it. They just live their

[39] cells in cerebral cortex are never replaced...

[40] while most cells are regenerated, the processes involved become progressively unreliable over time. In particular, the DNA carrying the instructions for cell processes becomes damaged, eventually preventing any more cell division. The result is the increasing level of decrepitude we call ageing.

[41] This is a fascinating subject and if you want to look into it further then the phrases to research are "telomerase" and "shortening of chromosomes."

brief lives to the maximum. Even in their later years, when their coats have lost their glossy sheen and their limbs can't run like they used to, right until the very end, they don't ever lose their zest for life. They are all still puppies at heart.

Most people's 'traditional' retirement lasts twice as long as the entire life expectancy of our canine companions. We would all do well to remember this and embrace the time we are gifted, rather than bemoan the human ageing process. The speed of ageing and the lifespan of the human species truly is a gift.

This canine time context is just the tip of the iceberg. Domestic dogs get to be positively ancient when you compare them to some other species. The humble mayfly has the unenviable record of having the shortest lifespan on earth. Mayflies are known as 'one-day insects' because their life lasts only for 24 hours.

Next time you are about to moan about how old you look or feel, think about your lot compared with that of some of our friends in the animal world. What can you do, experience or achieve in the **next decade** (a dog's life span). What are you going to do with **today** (a mayfly's lifespan?)

"Men are born soft and supple; dead they are stiff and hard. Plants are born tender and pliant; dead they are brittle and dry. Thus whoever is stiff and inflexible is a disciple of death. Whoever is soft and yielding is a disciple of life. The hard and the stiff will be broken. The soft and supple will prevail."

LAO TZU

This applies to your thinking as well as your body

Why do some people appear to age better than others?

A recent research project in Denmark used a sample group of twins to provide almost genetically identical subjects. This clever approach enabled a meaningful comparison of the impact of environmental factors on ageing. The findings were extremely encouraging, well at least to a point. They demonstrated that longevity is only 20% inherited and actually 80% is the result of 'environmental factors,' that is lifestyle. However, this situation only prevails up to the age of around 85.

Living healthily beyond 85 then appears to come down as much to inheriting the right genes as living a healthy lifestyle, with the ratio changing to roughly 50:50. Still pretty good odds though to make healthy living a pretty compelling life choice.

When it comes to health and dealing with ageing, there are two complimentary strategies that every aspiring Rock Star retiree can utilise:

1. Keeping up appearances (a real life Rock Star's agent might call this protecting your image rights).

2. Healthy ageing — you can't stop the ageing process itself, but you can certainly influence things by creating a healthy eating regime and living environment.

So let's tackle the subject of Rock Star image first.

How should we age?

As we have already observed, real life rock stars approach the inevitability of ageing in a multitude of ways. Denial, self-destruction, super healthy living etc. They also sometimes revert to image consultants, specialist make-up artists, cosmetic surgery, favourable lighting and, of course, air brushing of photographs or film footage to ensure they are conveyed in the most youthful way possible. While your face, voice or public image may not be the key to your future income stream and your ego may not be quite as large or as fragile, the fundamental choices you have are the same:

★ We can speed up the ageing process by abusing our body and living a toxic lifestyle.

★ We can give in to nature and get plumper, greyer and more hairy!

★ We can speed up the ageing process by 'thinking' old.

★ We can get the most from our body by looking after it with good nutrition and sleep levels.

★ We can 'cover up' or hide the signs of ageing to make the most of what we have and the age we are.

★ We can make the most of what we have by 'thinking' young'.

It is safe to say that most people will aspire to the last 3 optimal ageing options.

We want to look after the body in which we reside to get the best performance from it over the long-term.

★ Rather than to simply surrender passively to the ageing process, we want our appearance to be as attractive and youthful as possible for as long as possible via good dressing and grooming.

★ We want to remain young at heart, to keep our thinking youthful and optimistic, irrespective of how many miles we have on the clock, or of how age has physically manifested itself on our body.

The importance of sleep to long term mental capability

It is no great secret that sleep is essential for healthy living. We don't need scientists, or doctors, to tell us that a lack of sleep is bad for us. At some point in our lives, we have all felt the short-term effects of sleep deprivation. Miss out on sleep and the human mind quickly becomes clouded, with the ability to think, concentrate and react greatly diminished. These adverse effects on brain function put us in obvious short-term danger, leaving us at risk when driving and in jeopardy of making poor decisions while sleep-deprived. Yet scientists have recently discovered something we did not know; neglecting sleep consistently may have major **long-term** consequences too.

Like all of the body's other organs, the brain has an extensive network of blood vessels to supply oxygen and nutrients to fuel the cells that it is made up of. However, the other organs are served by a second, parallel network of vessels — the lymphatic system — designed to remove waste from between the cells and return it to the blood stream for disposal. For a reason that is not yet fully explained, but possibly down to the limited space inside our already densely packed rigid skulls, the brain evolved **externally** to the lymphatic system utilised by all the other organs. As a result, waste is dealt with in a different way. The brain pumps cerebrospinal fluid (CSF), using the outside of the existing blood vessels to flush through the spaces between the brains cells. Whether you are still fully with me or not, the detail of the biology does not matter. The key thing to understand is that the brain's unique way of dealing with waste disposal only functions **during the sleep cycle**.

When the brain goes to sleep, the brain cells appear to shrink in some way to allow the CSF fluid to rush between them, washing away the waste (a bit like colonic irrigation for the brain!) So the bottom line (no pun intended) is that if you don't get enough sleep, your brain does not benefit from its normal cleansing cycle. Insufficient sleep over a sustained period of time leads to a build-up of plaque of the brain's main 'waste' products, a protein called amyloid-beta. Amyloid-beta plaques are thought to be a major contributing factor towards Alzheimer's disease. I write this as dementia has just officially overtaken heart disease as the number one cause of death in the UK. Neglect your long-term sleep at your peril!

CASE STUDY:

The Rock Star Wife

I once had a client, (we will call her Mrs B), whose personal sense of identity, to an extreme level, revolved around her physical appearance. I genuinely have no idea of her age. She could have been 50 or she could have been 70. I have not seen her for a good few years and although I am not a betting man, I would stake my house on the fact that she will not have changed a bit! She was simply fascinating to behold, one of those people with a face you can't help but stare at, examine and re-examine in detail. This was because her face was impossible to 'read' and 'classify' in the way that, as humans, we normally do.

Mrs B was without doubt, the best groomed woman I have ever met. The embodiment of the classic rock star wife (although in this case, she was married to a 'business' rock star, rather than a musical one). She had gorgeous glossy hair, magnificent manicured nails, perfect pearly teeth, and a long slim body to show off her incredible wardrobe. Her flawless white face was so heavily made up that it is best described as a mature western woman's take on a Japanese geisha girl. However, although she was extremely well presented, it was totally impossible to tell whether she was, or indeed had ever been, naturally beautiful.

Mr and Mrs B appeared to be genuinely very happy together; an equal couple where she was fully involved in all of the major decisions for his business. On the occasions I met her alone, she seemed very happy in her own skin — although what that skin really looked like under her cosmetic cocoon I have no idea. However, it was her mannerisms, rather than her make-up, that really made her stand out. For the average human being, it takes 26 facial muscles to smile and 62 to frown. When Mrs B smiled, she only used around 10 facial muscles. An extensive use of Botox and probably more than one face lift, meant that only her mouth still retained the ability to move — above her lips everything remained completely tight and static. Indeed her default position seemed to be a Mona Lisa-like, wistful smile. This naturally meant that a frown requiring a further 52 muscles was totally out of the question. Yet when you think about Mrs B's predicament, while at times she seemed a little peculiar, not being able to frown is not necessarily a bad side effect to have.[21]

Whilst she seems happy, Mrs B also reminds us that an obsession with physical appearance and too strong an appetite to defy ageing can lead to extreme measures with extreme results. Ultimately, whilst we can make the best of what we have and where we are in the circle of life, too much emphasis on holding back the tide can lead to people becoming almost a caricature[22] and this is not the type of Rock Star Retiree that you want to be.

CASE STUDY:

Pizarro's barber: A Grooming Case Study From History!

Earlier in the book, perhaps rather controversially, I included Francisco Pizarro as an example of an individual who achieved great things at a late stage in his career. There is one further tale from this same Conquistadors era that I learned about during a visit to Peru back in 2000 that merits mention. It is a unique historical reference to the effects of personal grooming on our state of mind and wellbeing!

---

[21] If you have ever been on customer training course, or have had training in how to answer the phone, you are always told to smile when you answer – whatever facial expression you wear is supposed to come through in your voice. This begs the question, if it is harder to frown – are you happier?

[22] I also do not envy Mr B's task of waiting around in the morning for Mrs B to get ready to go out!

In the year 1532, Pizaro's invading army progressed deeper and deeper into inland Peru, looting and pillaging as they went. With each advancing mile towards the interior, they were watched ever more closely by Indian scouts. To the Incas, the appearance of the Spaniards was exotic. They had pale skin, facial hair and were extremely tall. On appraisal of the Spanish weaponry and military capability, the South Americans were impressed by the Spanish steel swords and armour. They were also particularly taken by the size, speed and agility of their hundred odd horses as the only beasts of burden available to the Incas were much smaller and more limited llamas. However, despite their advanced weaponry and impressive steeds, the Spanish invaders were deemed not to pose a genuine threat on the basis that their numbers were so few compared with the hundreds of thousands of battle-hardened foot soldiers at the command of the Inca king Atahualpa. There was a final unexpected observation too. One particular Spaniard stood out from the rest as having particularly motivational qualities. This individual was not Pizzaro, or one of his key generals; astonishingly, the Indian scouts had singled out a low ranking individual, more tradesman than leader or warrior.

On reporting back to their king, the Inca scouts' recommendation was to kill all but one of the Spanish and to take their horses which they realized could be bred to provide the Incas with a new much faster means of transport. Unfortunately for the Incas none of this came to pass, because the wily old Pizzaro rode his luck, played dirty and took the initiative by tricking and capturing the unarmed, complacent Inca king who had underestimated the threat and left himself poorly guarded.

However, it is the identity of the man the Incas had planned to spare that is fascinating to me, it was the Spaniards' barber! The Inca scouts had perceived that he appeared to have some mystical, morale-boosting powers on the other men in the invaders' company. They noted that whenever the troops went into his tent to have their hair cut or their beards trimmed, they came away, not only looking better, but they also seemed much happier and more jovial. Not much more is documented about the Spanish barber.

Perhaps he was a very cheerful soul or a natural wit, but I suspect that this is a very ancient account of how a simple decent haircut and a bit of grooming can have a strong impact on our mood and immediate sense of wellbeing.

For every aspiring Rock Star retiree, the objective is to be able to look in the mirror and feel that we are young for our age and can feel satisfied that we are living a decent lifestyle and making the best of what we have been given. No regrets remember.

Ageing goes way beyond the simple physical process. There are two very different aspects to the ageing process: Physical ageing and mental ageing (and by this I do not mean the physical health of the brain, I mean the 'outlook' of the person.)

The human brain and body co-exist and are totally interdependent. One cannot live without the other. Yet at the same time it is perfectly possible to have an old mind in a young body or the reverse, a young mind in an older body!

When it comes to our bodies, there is no question that our younger adult bodies are superior and preferable to our middle-age and later age versions, they are more flexible, stronger, faster, more reliable and more resilient. Yet when it comes to the brain/mind, it is not quite so simple.

When I was in the prime of my physical condition (perhaps my early to mid-20s) my mind had some very good features: I was optimistic and perhaps a little idealistic, but I was also very inexperienced. I was something of a late starter and I actually did not know very much about the world, or myself; as a consequence, I was quite insecure. As I write this book at the age of 43, I remain optimistic and hopeful for the future, but I understand the world and my place in it so much better. I am also much more comfortable in my own skin.

Would I swap my old inexperienced mind for my current one — absolutely not!

From my research into this subject, I know that this view is far from universally held. There are plenty of middle-aged and older people who have become more cynical and pessimistic than their younger selves.

Now let me ask you the question. If you had the option of having a young brain in an older body or an older brain in a young body which one would you take? I suppose to allow you to choose properly, I should define what is meant by old mind and old body.

By old mind, I mean your personality and outlook, and to some extent mental capability, by old body, I mean your physical form showing obvious signs of ageing and a deterioration in function, perhaps also reduced mobility and strength.

Would you like to be a more optimistic, happy and positive person? Would you like there to be more good news in your world for you to celebrate? It is a pretty safe bet that your answer to these two questions is a resounding yes! The next lesson could be the most important thing you have ever read. It is something that genuinely has the power to transform your life.

ROCK STAR ASSESSMENT:

Take a minute to think about which one best describes you?
Are you a young mind in an old body (aka Mick Jagger)
or are you more like the late Amy Winehouse at the height of
her fame (young body, old mind)? [23]

---

[23] There are of course lots of other options too. You could be a young mind in a young body, or worst of all an old mind in an old body and many things in between. I suppose technically I am actually a young mind in a middle aged body!

LESSON 5 SUMMARY

Ageing is an entirely natural and inevitable process.

Contrary to many people's perception, most elements of our bodies don't wear out over time. Instead the majority of cells that make up our bodies go through a continuous cycle of replacement and renewal. It is thought that each time cells are copied and replaced, tiny defects in the copying process lead to a deterioration. These flaws amplified over time are what lead to a deterioration in the form and function of all parts of our physical body, the process we call ageing.

Compared with many other species our aging process is extremely slow and we are gifted with significantly longer lives. Knowing that a mayfly lives only for a single day is a good way to remember to seize each and every day and to stop worrying about what age we are. Every day is a gift.

Why some people appear to age better/slower than others is a complex question. Recent research has shown that up to the age of 85, how we age is 80% down to environmental factors (e. g. lifestyle) and only 20% genetic.

There is currently no cure for ageing, but there are 3 ways that as aspiring Rock Star Retirees we can face ageing in a positive way:

★ Make the most of our appearance by good grooming and masking (e. g. dying hair, good make up, removing unsightly hair (Simon Cowell famously has his hands waxed!).

★ Live a healthy lifestyle via good diet and exercise.

★ Maintain a young mind and outlook.

To some extent, all 3 of these strategies interconnect and reinforce each other. The Pizarro Barber story illustrated how the ancient Inca civilisation noted the psychological boost of good grooming. Look good, feel good, feel good, feel young. Likewise (as we saw in the previous lesson about natural drugs), exercise releases feel good endorphins that make us feel good, positive and young.

The Rock Star Wife case study (featuring the Botox queen) warned us of the perils of taking anti-ageing grooming a step too far.

Ageing is not all bad, personalities can deepen and our understanding of what is important in the world and where we fit into the scheme of things can lead to greater confidence, self-esteem and in fact happiness.

Whilst it is not news that a good night's sleep is an important part of any healthy living regime. Looking beyond the short-term effects of sleep deprivation, new research has shown that sleep is essential to allow the brains unique cleansing system to function. In the light of these new findings, it is now believed that sleep deprivation leads to long-term damage to the brain, by allowing plaques to build up. It is these plaques and the damage they cause to the surrounding brain tissue that are thought to lead to Alzheimer's disease and dementia. Time to forego some of those Rock Star all night sessions and replace them with a nice cup of camomile? Maybe, but make sure that you don't go too far with this. Playing it safe can lead to an old mind (in terms of outlook.)

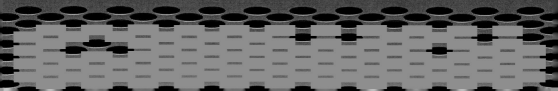

LESSON 6

ROCK STAR FOCUS

LIVING OUR LIVES THROUGH A LENS (WHY LIFE IS NOT QUITE WHAT IT SEEMS!)

This is Major Tom to Ground Control
I'm stepping through the door
And I'm floating in a most peculiar way
And the stars look very different today
For here
Am I sitting in a tin can
Far above the world
Planet Earth is blue
And there's nothing I can do

DAVID BOWIE — Space Oddity

We think of the physical world as a pretty straightforward place to exist in. While we may not recall our high school physics lessons in any great detail, we understand that the physical world adheres to a series of rules, the laws of physics. We know that gravity dictates which way is up and down and that our senses allow us to 'comprehend', navigate and interact with the physical world. Our eyes take in light which bounces off physical objects to allow us to see. Our ears are built to capture sound and enable us to hear and interact with the world around us. Our other senses allow us to touch, taste and smell. All make sense so far? Still with me? Good, because this is where it starts to get really interesting.

The problem with our normal understanding of the way we view and interact with the world is that we assume that our physical senses (eyes, ears etc) are simply relaying the images and sounds from the real world to our brains in full and that we are seeing the physical world exactly as it is. The reality is that your brain is deceiving you and distorting the real world around you **almost all the time**. The world around you as you see it is an abridged, interpreted and distorted view of the reality.

Don't believe me? Don't worry, I will prove it to you in a minute, but first let me explain why this great deception takes place and once the penny has dropped, how you can use it to your very great advantage in making your world a much happier place to be in.

First let's deal with the why, in terms of why is our brain giving us a distorted view of the world?

Christmas shopping hell

Frank (our Rock Star Retirement anti-hero from the introduction) is walking through a large shopping centre in Bradford on a bustling Saturday morning on the final shopping weekend before Christmas. Whilst he is very fond of his family, he is seriously regretting offering to go Christmas shopping with his sister, Sarah and his niece and nephew. His arms are linked with the children's to ensure they don't get lost and as a consequence, it is proving extremely difficult to make any sort of progress through the crowds. He is also burdened by a number of heavy purchases and the narrow handles of the plastic bags he is carrying are really digging in and hurting his hands. Christmas music is playing on the audio system and there are a hundred or more conversations going on around him among the dynamic throng of shoppers. To complete the cacophony, there are buskers and a brass band on the street and each store he walks into seems to be playing the same Christmas compilation soundtrack. He passes a travel agent and scans the Christmas package deals longingly. He vows that next year he will avoid this crazy Western consumer culture by going abroad.

The wind chill factor is making the air temperature outside feel freezing. Every time Frank walks into a shop, he gets blasted by the super-hot climate control and has to immediately take off his coat and jumper to avoid overheating. As well as carrying the garments he has just shed, he is also burdened by the children's coats and jumpers. He catches a fleeting glance of himself as he passes; he looks like an overburdened ruddy-faced cricket umpire-come-porter. Every time he leaves a shop, he has to put all the bags down and layer himself and the children up again. The contrasting temperatures are so extreme that he has noticed other less well wrapped up children crying due to the cold. He readjusts his mental image of himself and drops the cricket umpire analogy. He decides that this feels a bit like a cross between the school family dressing up race and a contestant in some crazy Japanese endurance game show. Neither mental image brings him any cheer — this is like his own personal hell.

His mood is made worse when he overhears a neighbouring conversation about the football. Despite his Yorkshire roots, he is actually a Liverpool supporter and today is the biggest match of them all, Liverpool versus Manchester United. He would have dearly loved to watch the match on the television but family duty called.

Normally he would keep track of the score on his smart phone, but the shopping centre is so overcrowded that the network can't cope and there is no coverage. However, he has become adept at tuning into other people's conversations to keep track of the score — and keeping an eye out to catch a few moments of action at the occasional electronics store he passes.

Frank heard on the news yesterday that many retailers take half of their annual sales and profits from the Christmas season[24] and so they are all going all out with promotions to attract his attention. He is hungry and the bread smell from the Subway franchise and the sweet cookie store smell are calling. He is also tired and yet his sister really wants to get to the knitting shop to buy great aunt Edna that angora wool she loves to work with.

Now one of the children needs to go to the bathroom again and his sister has just found a jacket to try on and wants his opinion. He has that conversation again about who they are supposed to be shopping for and how squeezed **her** budget is at this time of year. This does not help improve the mood. His mobile phone just rang in his pocket and having checked to see who the missed call was from, but unable to do anything because the coverage has gone again, the store security guard seems to be paying him far too much attention. Oh God! Does he think he just slipped something into his pocket? Doesn't he realise it was just his phone? He swallows hard and the fact that he feels like he looks guilty just compounds the problem. That guy in the Father Christmas suit looks strangely familiar. Just when he thought it could not get any worse, he notices that little Johnny has just wet himself.

I think you get the picture! This scene, or something similar, is played out and experienced by millions of people every year, which is probably why Internet shopping is increasing in popularity.

I chose this scene to illustrate just how complicated and overwhelming the world around us can be. At any one time during our daily activities (even during much less frenetic scenarios than the one just outlined) our mind is bombarded with millions of pieces of sensory input from the physical environment around us.

Sights, sounds, smells, tastes and feelings are continually being inputted into our 'brain' system, but only a tiny fraction of this can actually be handled by our conscious minds.

[24] Centre For Retail Research, Nottingham UK

Another example of how our brains try to make sense of things around us, are optical illusions. Many of us love these diagrams but they show just how differently your brain can see things to that of your friend, partner of family member.

Take a look at the picture below.

Do you see two fish or a face looking left?

Our brain will try to make sense of what it sees out of what it knows, but also adding in our own emotions.

ROCK STAR TIP:

What you focus on gets amplified,
So focus on life's sweet music

To allow us to make sense of the wold, our brains have to filter some things out to help us cope and survive.

This filtering process is the job of your Reticular Activating System (RAS). As an easy analogy, you can think of it as being a bit like a bouncer for your brain. Your RAS filters out information you don't need and focuses in on what you do, so that you are able to tune into the things that are both most valuable (or what you think is most valuable) and most threatening to you.

Is there something valuable around like an attractive person, or perhaps your favourite food? What about that enormous bull on the other side of the field you and your family are trying to cross? RAS tunes into it and it gets your conscious attention. But beyond these base, lower brain drivers it also applies equally to higher brain activity and the associated, self-actualising aspects of your life. Understanding your RAS and applying this knowledge can make a significant difference to your outlook and your life.

The applications are endless, but the key thing that you need to be aware of and understand is that your brain does not show you an exact copy of the world that is going on around you. It interprets what it thinks you need and want to be seeing. It picks out the parts of your input that it thinks are the most relevant.

This is why focusing on what you want and not on what you don't want, is so crucial. When you are focused on what you want, your RAS eventually leads you to find the solution. It also can be a big influence on how you see the world. If you have a positive outlook and feel that the world is generally a decent place, then your brain will help to reinforce this by focusing on good news stories and positive people. If you are currently more of a pessimist and feel that the world is a dangerous, bad place, your brain will focus on this and reinforce this in what it focuses your conscious attention on.

All of us would benefit from a more positive and more productive outlook and the brilliant news is that, although the core lower brain focus is more or less hard wired, the rest is not. The way you view the world and what you pay attention to is something that you have effectively programmed through the course of your life and by your life's experiences to date. And now that you understand how it works, it is therefore something you can genuinely alter and 're-programme'.

Start small if necessary. Train yourself to expect good things. When you wake up each morning tell yourself that it is going to be a good day, a day filled with opportunity. When you begin thinking like this you will truly start to see more positive events and more opportunities. The truth is that they were always there, your brain was just not tuned into them. Reinforce this by reflecting each night before you go to sleep on something positive or good that happened.

Get into the habit of thinking about the good and not focusing on the bad. Learn to play the positive mentality game, for every piece of bad news that you hear, find a positive perspective and try to put it into context. When you hear about a robbery or break in, remember that for every anti-social or criminal activity reported, there are probably a thousand good deeds by decent people with social consciousness taking place at the same time which are all going totally unreported.

As I have said before, you can't necessarily choose what life throws at you, but you can choose how to react and deal with it. This is why some people seem to get on in life better than others. Armed with this knowledge and with further research, application and practice, you too can see the world as a better place.

As we get older, it can be extremely easy to get set in our ways. We see life the way we choose to see it, via input channels that we become comfortable with and self-select. Think about your music taste. You may occasionally add a few new artists to your music collection (perhaps influenced by your own children), but it is very likely that most of the music you listen to harks back to your teens and your 20s. You probably also read the same newspaper and listen to, or watch the same news bulletins, week after week, year after year.

The problem with occupying these comfort zones is that it can lead to a distorted view of the world as presented by the media you choose. For example, here in the UK, we have national newspapers aligned to different political parties. The Daily Mail, for example, is aligned with the Conservative party (capitalist and right of the political centre ground) while the Guardian is much more aligned with the Labour party (left of centre) with a socialist leaning. On any given day, you could read an article in each of these two publications and be presented with a very different interpretation on what actually happened. With news freely available online, it is easier than ever to get different takes on world events from different sources.

My first port of call is normally the excellent BBC website, but from time to time, I will check out coverage and opinion via the International New York Times and also the New Zealand Herald. This allows me to understand world events from different perspectives and helps to keep me sharp and objective.

When reading something, it always pays to apply a degree of objective cynicism. A great technique is to ask yourself questions and decide the agenda behind the article.

The classic examples of this trend are so called scientific studies into different foodstuffs. One minute margarine is good for you due to its low saturated fat content; this will be quickly countered by another study which reveals that butter is better for you because it does not contain the harmful man-made compounds found in margarine. When you look into who commissioned these types of studies, you will find that more often than not, they have been bankrolled by a vested interest that is a leading margarine or butter producer with a specific agenda of finding data to support the health benefits of the product and the sole objective of generating more sales.

Newsreaders will always perceive that they live in dangerous times. The reality is that in most years bee stings, deer collisions, ignition of nightwear, and other mundane accidents kill more Americans than terrorist attacks.

Why is the world always "more dangerous than it has ever been", even as a greater majority of humanity dies of old age?

The only sound way to appraise the state of the world is to *count*. How many violent acts has the world seen compared with the number of opportunities? And is that number going up or down? As Bill Clinton likes to say, "Follow the trend lines, not the headlines." Take this approach and you will quickly see that the trend lines are much more encouraging than a news junkie would ever guess.

Go on a positive 'mental' diet

Just as the food you eat has an impact on your body, negative or positive, so does the diet you give your brain. If you allow too much negative input, you are liable to have a negative, or even pessimistic, world view. If you selectively control your diet of mental input to a primarily positive one — books and articles that are educational, motivational or inspirational — then your outlook will naturally follow suit.

One of the downsides of modern society is our cultural obsession with superficial appearance. In a planet of billions of people, we hold up a handful of the most beautiful celebrities as the aspiration. These beautiful creatures are often groomed, starved (on the latest extreme diet fad) and tortured (by a personal trainer) to within an inch of their lives! We are then bombarded from all angles by adverts showing images of these flawlessly airbrushed men and women and how the promoted product they are peddling can make you more like them. These people are not real, they are caricatures, often with very little real talent, genuine gravitas or 'soul'. Yet because they are beamed into our consciousness via the internet, television and billboards, we start to think of them as the norm and as a benchmark against which we compare ourselves, our worth and value.

As a consequence, far too many people dwell on the ageing process, often from an incredibly young age. They spend too much time worrying and not enough time living. It is important to remember how blessed we are to have been born and to be living in this unprecedentedly affluent and opportune moment in human history.

"Don't let yesterday take up too much of today"
WILL ROGERS

Be careful what you wish for. Going back to those beautiful airbrushed caricatures, we need to start to judge people, not by how they look, but actually by how happy they are. The truth is that most modern celebrities are messed up. Beauty and fame via the caricature their management has them become makes them lose touch with reality. Fame can be like a drug, the more they have, the more they need and when inevitably their moment to shine diminishes, they fall into depression. It is no coincidence that so many icons commit suicide, die of alcohol or drug abuse, or lose their fortune through gambling or other attempts to seek alternative highs.

"We either make ourselves miserable or we make ourselves strong. The amount of work is the same"
CARLOS CASTANEDA, AUTHOR

Choose your source material carefully

For thousands of years, people have peddled myths and stories about miraculous age-defying artefacts and places. From the Fountain of Youth, the waters of Vilcabamba and the Holy Grail, to the ambrosia of the gods, the philosopher's stone and the elixir of life, these tales span almost all cultures and ages.

Our age is no different. Ageing is a universal trend and naturally people have always sought a 'cure' and as the process sets in, they will often ignore their instinctive judgement and throw good money at something suspect "just in case."

At a recent over 50s show I attended, there was a so called professor selling a miraculous anti-ageing, energy-boosting remedy.[25] When I looked into it, it appeared to be nothing more than a caffeine-based stimulant. You have to ask the question, if this really was a genuine anti-ageing product how many billions of dollars would the big multinational biotechnology corporations have paid him for it? Instead there he was personally having to pedal it directly to customers. Yet at least this guy has the courage to stand up in front of people to sell his wares. It was a pretty small-scale operation, and perhaps his customers did derive some form of benefit from the placebo effect of just taking it. The real Wild West for this sort of thing is now the online marketplace. The Google search engine exploded onto the online scene on the back of a fantastically clever search algorithm to help people find the most relevant information online as quickly as possible. However, Google is a corporation with financial objectives and these days there appears to be an increased blurring between 'paid for searches' (i. e. advertisements) and 'organic' content (searches coming up because they have the most relevant, most authentic content for the search terms). In other words, companies can pay Google to get customers' eyeballs on their products for certain keyword combinations, irrespective of whether or not the product actually matches the description of "best" or "cheapest" or "most reliable" etc.

And to a certain degree, it is possible for the same companies to buy the non-paid for 'organic' slots too. Healthcare companies with anti-ageing products frequently hire PR agencies and pay experts to conduct research that ultimately is designed with an agenda to promote their product as the best in the market. These reports are then of course

---

[25] Some of the claimed benefits made me chuckle because they were reminiscent of the early medicinal features suggested by Coca Cola's founder.

published and distributed widely online and represent some of the content that you will find when you ignore the paid for adverts and search the organic search engine results.

The following post from Mark Brown distributed via social media channels demonstrates this point brilliantly.

The trouble with quotes on the Internet is that you can never know if they are genuine.

Abraham Lincoln

It is not all bad though! There is plenty of superb, credible information to be found online too. You just need to remember to be analytical and selective about how and where you go to source a balanced view of the world. It keeps the mind young and active to apply an objective policing of your window on the world.

Common Rock Star Retiree thinking

A significant number of my most successful, happy clients feel positive about themselves to the degree that they feel they are in control of their lives and their ability to achieve and maintain inner peace of mind. There will always be bumps in the road, but they know and accept that they can only do their best. They point out that it is not **what** happens to them, but **how they think about it** which is important. It is their **thinking** that stimulates their feelings and emotions, positive or negative. It is their ability to manage the inevitable day-to-day stresses of their lives that is a keystone of their successful Rock Star Retirement. **In other words, your life is what you think it is**. Take a moment to reflect this. This knowledge, if applied can totally transform your entire life.

Developing a Rock Star Retiree mindset

A pretty obvious place to start in my quest to replicate my Rock Star Retirement heroes, was to go straight to the horse's mouth and to ask them how they did it. Now this lot by nature are a pretty modest, humble group, so the initial reaction was along the lines of "I'm not that special", or "I am not sure I deserve to be classed as a rock star retiree." They are also a pretty kind, caring and enthusiastic bunch, so once I managed to get them talking about themselves, they became extremely animated, passionate and quite frankly hard to keep up with during my note taking!

From the case studies provided, we already know that most Rock Star retirees were ordinary people, following a conventional life plan until a catalyst, or stimulus, in their life made them take stock and choose a different path. It also turns out that before this event, they were very normal people who thought in conventional ways. They were ordinary folk, just drifting along with the stresses and strains that our media tell us are part and parcel of our modern age. In re-evaluating and rede-signing their destination, they also went through a process of re-evaluating and redesigning their mindset. In a nutshell, they changed their thinking. To facilitate this process, they had to change old engrained habits, and remove undesirable stimuli, including, spending less time around negative people. Another successful strategy advocated widely by my cohort was actively seeking out and spending more time around positive people of a similar mind-set (other Rock Star Retirees.)

People are not born with a Rock Star Retiree mind-set, it is something that has to be actively worked at and developed on a continuous basis.

One or two of the smartest people (such as Plato, as you will learn in a few pages time), figured out how to do this themselves, but the vast majority, including me, simply borrowed, collated and adapted other people's thought strategies.

How did they develop their mindset?

Think about your window on the world. How big is it? Is the glass distorted, or does it provide a clear image of the world? The truth is that it is a big world out there and to some extent, we all live in our own unique little bubble. Remember RAS? Our brain acts as a filter and tunes in to what it thinks is important in the world we inhabit. But crucially, the input is already filtered before the RAS filters it further! Your mind and the senses providing input into it, can only take in what your bubble allows them to.

If you think about your day-to-day life, you will probably quickly realise that you exist inside a pretty small bubble. We are often creatures of habit. We go to work in the same place every day. We listen to the same radio station, watch the same TV programmes, frequent the same websites and interact with the same people. As thinking beings, we are affected by what we do, say, hear, watch and listen to. The environment we exist in — before our RAS filters it further — is already filtered by the view from within our bubble. The problem for many people is that they do not let their bubble expand its and their horizons.

As part of your Rock Star Retirement journey, it is important to ensure that you have a decent understanding of what the world **really** looks like. You have to let your bubble go to different places. I would love to claim credit for this brilliant insight into the way we view our world, but unfortunately someone beat me to this, by just a fraction under 2,500 years!

Rock star philosophy: 'The Allegory of the Cave' by Plato

The 'Allegory of the Cave' is a hypothesis put forward by the Greek philosopher Plato, concerning human perception. Plato claimed that *knowledge gained through the senses is no more than opinion and that, in order to have real knowledge, we must gain it through philosophical reasoning.* In this clever allegory, Plato distinguishes between people who mistake sensory knowledge for the truth and people who really do see the truth. It very much applies to the Rock Star Retirement philosophy and goes like this:

Imagine a cave in which there are three prisoners. The prisoners are tied to some rocks, their arms and legs are bound and their head is tied so that they cannot look at anything but the stone wall in front of them. The prisoners have been here since birth and have never seen outside of the cave.

Behind the prisoners is a fire, and between them is a raised walkway. People outside the cave walk along this, sometimes carrying things on their heads, on their backs, or in their arms. These things include animals, plants and other objects of all kinds of shapes and sizes.

Imagine that you are one of the prisoners. You cannot look at anything behind or to the side of you. You must look at the wall in front of you, this is the limit of your visual bubble. When people walk along the walkway, you can see the shadows of their silhouettes and the silhouettes of the objects they are carrying cast on to the wall. If you had never seen the real objects ever before, you would believe that the shadows of objects were 'real.'

Plato suggests that the prisoners would begin a 'game' of guessing which shadow would appear next. If one of the prisoners were to correctly guess, the others would praise him as clever and say that he was a master of nature (i.e. he had a great understanding of the world).

One of the prisoners then escapes from their bindings and leaves the cave. Outside of his normal frame of reference 'bubble,' he is shocked at the world he discovers outside of the cave and does not believe it can be real. As he becomes used to his new surroundings, he realises that his former view of reality was wrong. He begins to understand his new world, and sees that the sun is the source of life and goes on an intellectual journey where he discovers beauty and meaning. He sees that his former life, and the guessing game they played is useless. The prisoner returns to the cave, to inform the other prisoners of his findings. They do not believe him and threaten to kill him if he tries to set them free.

The cave context change in reality: Liz's story

Perhaps my quick philosophy 101 lesson felt a bit abstract, so it's time to bring us back to the here and now. The point is that for many people, achieving a much happier existence, requires very few physical changes to their world at all. It may just take a mental context shift in their mindset to appreciate what they already have: a realisation that there is no need to chase the dream that the media pushes with fame, status or materialism the ultimate aspiration.

"Nothing is quite as important as you think it is, while you are thinking about it", according to a fortune cookie enjoyed at a Chinese restaurant in Manchester's China Town on my wife's birthday in February 2015.

One of my work colleagues Liz made this mental metamorphosis in dramatic fashion. Almost overnight, she went from being one of the world's biggest moaners possessing a textbook example of a victim mentality, to one of the warmest, kindest, most pragmatic and opti-mistic souls I have ever had the pleasure of knowing. A few months after her epiphany, when it became apparent that this spectacular change for the better really was going to be a permanent change, I plucked up the courage to compliment her new mindset and to enquire what had brought this about.

It transpired that there were two external events that catalysed this change. The first was when one of her friends suffered the loss of a new-born baby. Historically, much of Liz's moaning had been about the demands and rigours of having three young children to raise. In the context of what had befallen her friend, she now felt embarrassed about her comparably trivial grievances and instead felt blessed to have three beautiful, healthy, active, energetic and demanding children.

The second stimulus came quickly after the first, when the partner of one of her other friends became chronically ill. Liz suddenly realised that health is a gift that can quickly be taken away and that she needed to count her blessings while she had them. It gave her a new apprecia-tion of her husband too, when she thought about what her friend must be going through and projected those feelings onto how she would feel if he became ill.

Liz did not actively go looking for these lessons, instead, they came to her, but she had the presence of mind to heed them. As a result, her life has dramatically changed for the better. The changes were not in a physical or monetary way that a financial adviser, or traditional retirement planner, could measure. The change was all in her head. She inhabits what is ostensibly exactly the same physical world, but the way she now sees things is completely different and she is significantly happier.

It would seem that before we choose our filters, first we need to see and understand the world for what it really is. We can speed this process up by moving our bubble and exploring the world and the stimuli that enters it — both physically and mentally.

Liz is an exceptional woman and her epiphany and seeming overnight transformation was unusual. For most people, including myself, it is an ongoing project.

A humble admission

As my long suffering wife will vouch, I am far from the finished article. I am certainly no great sage or oracle. I am as fundamentally flawed as any other human, but I can say with absolute certainty that my life has been far better empowered by what I have learnt, than if I had continued to think the way I used to and I am a better person for it. I am optimistic about the future, I have a plan, goals and a system and I am thoroughly enjoying the journey.

"Life moves pretty fast.
If you don't stop and look around once in a while,
you could miss it."
FERRIS BUELLER

LESSON 6: SUMMARY

Life through a Lens & How to Develop a Rock Star Mindset

Our window onto the world is a distorted one. In the modern digital age, we live in an environment awash with information. Social media platforms and blogging have suddenly made everyone a writer, a publisher and to some extent a journalist.

As a result, everyone is vying for attention (measured by the various audience metrics of, viewers, likes, shares, reposts, retweets, subscribers).

Standing out from the crowd and being heard has become more and more difficult and the problem has been compounded by the fact that people's attention spans are decreasing. This has led to a trend towards the sensationalised headline grabbing stories and sound bites dominating mainstream national media channels.

Unfortunately these stories are typically of a negative nature and are not detailed, balanced analytical pieces. Instead their authors state opinion as though it is fact.

If you hear the same incorrect messages being said loud enough and repeated often enough then there is a very real danger that they will start to sound real.

Throw genuinely contrived fake news into the mix, factor in the commercial agenda of search engines, the PR strategies of companies paying experts to produce positive research about their products and it truly becomes very difficult to see the wood for the trees in terms of:

★ Who we can trust
★ What is actually factual
★ Which things we genuinely need to be aware of
★ What the real world actually looks like.

Increasing specialisation within our jobs also means that we are living in smaller and smaller 'bubbles'; working from the same places, only interacting with specialists within our given niches and small circle of true friends and family. Being a specialist pays, but it also means that we pay less and less interest to the world outside our sector bubbles and see less and less of the real world.

To complicate matters, our brains also naturally give us a distorted view of the world. Our reticular activating system (RAS) only draws our conscious attention to things it believes are important to us and naturally seeking out data and input from the world to support existing beliefs.

This means that that we view the world through two separate lenses, each one only allowing parts of the reality to reach our brain. The quality of our view of the world is only as good as the input we allow inside and only as good as the quality of our brain's filter and how we process and 'think' about the information.

With too little thought, it is far too easy to fall into the trap of taking the information we receive at face value and starting to see the world as a bad and declining place.

It is therefore critical to choose your source material, your 'mental diet' very carefully. This is likely to involve changing television, radio and reading habits. And may require you to end interactions with any particularly negative people in your day to day life.

Plato's allegory of the cave showed us that the way we perceive the world is simply our interpretation and not necessarily the reality. It also warned of the danger of developing a Rock Star mind set. Challenging conventional mainstream thinking is likely to be met by significant resistance by those who are still under its spell.

"Nothing in life is as important as you think it is"

Liz's story vividly demonstrated in practice, how a shift in mindset can dramatically alter a person's world view and enjoyment and appreciation of their life, even when nothing physical has changed.

Maintaining the positive mental attitude of a Rock Star Retiree is an ongoing and continuous process. Being selective about what input you allow into your mind and how you choose to think about it takes dedication and commitment.

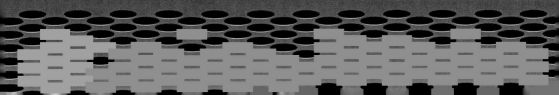

LESSON 7

ROCK STAR PRIORITIES

MANAGING YOUR CAREER

Oh how I'd love it girl, just you and me
Take the day and fly
But oh this job, it's got the best of me
Tell you why, tell you why

Somebody above is in a desperate state
Some kind of urgency, the kind that won't wait
I say tomorrow, he say today
And the man in my head well he tell me no way
Keep working
I got eight little fingers and only two thumbs
Will you leave me in peace while I get the work done
Can't you see I'm working

Chris Rea — Working on it

Following on from the first case study, the contrasting lives of Ian and Frank, I would now like to introduce you to two more couples whose lives have also panned out in dramatically different ways. However, this time, to protect them, I will substitute their real names.

By most conventional measures, the first couple are extremely successful, not quite at the 'Posh and Becks,' or 'Beyoncé and Jay Z' celebrity level, but they are doing very well. In reflection of this, I am going to call them the 'Go-getters.' In contrast, the second couple live by much more modest means, with far less outward signs of wealth and success. To reflect this, I will call them the 'Humbles.' Both couples are decent law-abiding citizens and both are good company. Here is a quick comparison of their early years:

COUPLE 1:
The 'Go-getters'

Both the same age, the Go-getters were born into a remote, rural community 2 hours' drive from the nearest town or city. Their village was picturesque, but isolated. They got to know each other at school and in their mid-teens, became child-hood sweet hearts, drawn together by a shared passion to escape the limited opportunities of their birthplace, and by fierce ambition and the lure and promise of big city life.

Despite attending different campuses hundreds of miles apart, their relationship survived the challenges and rigours that normally kill off long distance university relationships. Soon after graduating they moved to London, married and bought their first flat together.

They worked hard in their fledgling professional careers. Whilst their peers went to the pubs and clubs after work looking for Mr or Mrs right, the Go-getters having already found each other, were able to use their spare time to further their careers. Via networking and studying for additional qualifications, they quickly rose through the ranks to achieve high status and well remunerated positions within the City Of London at a very young age.

During these early career years, they enjoyed the fruits of their hard work, climbing the housing ladder, upgrading cars regularly and enjoying their disposable income on exotic overseas holidays, frequently flying first or business class.

Their most significant accomplishments (new jobs, pay rises, bonuses and new apartments) were very publically celebrated and during their first decade of marriage they threw some legendary parties.

Between their late 20's and up to their mid-30's they were blessed with 3 healthy children. With a growing family they naturally needed more space and they relocated from their 3 bedroom duplex river view apartment to 5 bedroom London town house South of the river, complete with a hot-tub and an extra bedroom for a nanny, purchased for close to a cool million pounds. True to form, they threw a memorable party to celebrate, literally whilst the paint was still drying on the freshly redecorated walls. In so many ways they were and are a golden couple, with so much to celebrate and be grateful for.

COUPLE 2:
The 'Humbles'

Mrs Humble is older than her husband. They got together when he was in his mid-20s and she was approaching 30. Just like the Go-getters, they are both bright and their careers got off to a good start. Mr Humble, who is both creative and technically gifted, started out as a web designer. His wife's job is both very specialist and vocational. Being older and having worked for longer, she was earning significantly more than her partner when they met, although this was never an issue for them. One consequence of them teaming up a little later in life, was that their first step on to the housing ladder was also later. By the time they bought their first home — a modest two bedroom Victorian terraced house — the Go-getters were already onto their 3rd step of the housing ladders — an apartment worth nearly 3 times as much as the Humbles new home.

Social events and house parties for the Humbles in their early years as a couple centred around traditional calendar events, such as birthdays and

Halloween, rather than a need to celebrate and share the fruits of their success. Some would argue that they had less achievements to celebrate, indeed while Mrs Humble's career continued on a fairly steady upward trajectory, her husband's did not. In his early 30s, due to a temporary health issue, he was forced to take several months off work. During this difficult time, he was shocked to find that his employers were both unsympathetic and unsupportive. With time to think, he had something of a crisis of conscience. After much reflection, he decided that the hard-nosed, over commercial focus of his employer, both to customers and staff, was not a culture he wanted to exist in. He also felt that compared to his wife's job, which made a genuine difference to people, his career was trivial and unfulfilling. They talked things through as a couple and did the maths. Knowing that if they were careful with their expenditure, they could afford to live on her wage alone, he resigned with no idea of what he was going to do next.

Exercise 1:

Which couple do you consider to be the most successful?

_____

Which couple do you think is the happiest?

_____

Which couple does your own approach to life most resemble?

_____

Which couple would you most like to be like?

_____

But as you probably already guessed, our story is not yet done. Let's take a look at the next phase of these two couple's lives:

COUPLE 1
'The Go-getters'—Part 2

As their success and career status rose higher, the Go-getters began to mix with an increasingly affluent circle of people and as a result, their context changed.

They began to compare themselves with people residing in multi-million pound homes and even people with more than one home. Having had a continuous upward curve of promotion and 'tangible' success from the start of their careers, they had become addicted to a life punctuated by status 'scores', salary increases and big city bonuses. Within the newest parts of their social circle, their 5 bedroom house in Clapham suddenly seemed very small and ordinary, not giving them the sense of satisfaction or achievement that it used to.

The Go-getters then learnt the hard way that early promotions and pay rises are much easier to obtain than later ones. Management and pay structures are pyramidal in nature, each time they ascended a step of the pyramid, the fewer the number of opportunities that remained above them and the harder they became to reach. The higher they aspired to go, the more of themselves they had to give to their jobs, with more overseas business travel and more 'unpaid' time input and the endurance of more stress.

Their house parties [and more child friendly barbecues] became fewer and less legendary. Like junkies they began to lose sight of the consequences of their relentless need for a status fix. The tipping point came when a global economic shock killed the stock market bull run that they had surfed so successfully and lucratively for so long. Their Big city bonuses evaporated overnight, but they still had a massive mortgage and expensive living costs and private school fees to service. Childcare duties became almost totally outsourced between their nanny during the week and relying on the goodwill of neighbours and some of their children's friend's parents for much of the weekends as they struggled to make ends meet.

Thankfully their marriage remained strong throughout, but relationships with neighbours and other key people who they relied on so heavily for free child-care deteriorated as they increasingly felt used and put on – many of them terminally. As well as having few friends left, they came to realise that they had missed out on significant chunks of their children's young lives to the point where they sometimes felt more like an uncle and aunt, than a father and mother.

In their relentless pursuit of their next fix of career and monetary success, their next status affirming executive car, the Go-getters had completely lost their way. Somewhere along the way, their dream had become a total nightmare.

COUPLE 2
'The Humbles'—Part 2

Now unemployed, but grateful for having such a supportive wife, Mr Humble dusted himself off and went back out into the world to find his true calling.

Keen to do something more meaningful and having recently come through tough times himself, he wondered if he could help others going through similar difficulties. His initial research led to him taking a course in counselling. This in turn led to voluntary work as a counsellor. He also busied himself at home with DIY projects, cooking, cleaning, gardening and generally turning their modest house into a beautiful family home. And with the nest now looking beautiful and their relationship stronger than ever, the Humbles were blessed with a beautiful baby daughter.

A sensitive and highly caring man, Mr Humble took to parenting brilliantly. They both did, but with mum established in a great career and earning good money, following her statutory maternity leave, it made sense for Dad to stay at home and this is how it remained.

When their daughter started school, Mr Humble went back to voluntary work, but was and is, still the first parent at the school gate when it is home time.

The Humbles continue to reside in their first house. They have never given a second thought to what other people think. If you ask them to describe what they do, he is a 'dad' and she is a 'teacher' but they are both so much more. Indeed to this day, I still don't actually know what Mrs Humble's real job title is!

Exercise 2:

Which couple do you **now** consider to be the most successful?

_____

Which couple do you **now** think is the happiest?

_____

Which couple does your own approach to life most resemble?

_____

Which couple would you most like to be like now?

_____

Materialism..

A cautionary note perhaps, but at all stages of our lives there is almost always a degree of compromise between the twin currencies of **time** and **money**. The problem is that so many people are getting the balance badly wrong. The Dalai Lama recently summed up the problems with our modern life-styles brilliantly:

> *"man sacrifices his health in order to make money.*
> *Then he sacrifices his pay to recuperate his health.*
> *After this he is so anxious about the future that*
> *he does not enjoy the present; the result being that*
> *he does not live in the present or the future;*
> *he lives as if he is never going to die,*
> *and then he dies never really having lived."*

Whilst known not to be materialistic, the Dalai Lama is bang on the money with this!

Yet in the Western World today, especially in Europe, which has many spectacularly generous cradle to grave state systems, if you are so inclined, it is possible to eke out a subsistence life-style without working at all. You would have to play the system, but in England for example you could get state housing, a weekly subsistence cash sum and free health-care.

Time rich, cash poor. Yet for most people this too is an unsatisfactory situation. Whilst these unemployed people may appear to live in a relatively stress free environment, this other extreme situation also leads to health issues. Social housing tends to be situated in more down market areas, areas with higher crime rates. Internally social housing is designed to provide shelter but little more. Those living purely on benefits may struggle to heat their home comfortably and a lack of money, job and no reason to get up in the morning is also not a healthy situation.

Materialism: A Different Perspective from an Altered Reality.

You wake up from a deep night's sleep and roll over to find your partner is not there. This is unusual as you are always the early riser, your partner hates mornings. Even more bizarrely, you walk around the house to find it completely devoid of the rest of your family too. No partner and 2 missing children! It is 8am on a Saturday morning, where on earth could they be? Perplexed and desperately trying to remember if they had something on early today that you have forgotten, you grab a coffee and switch on the TV. This is getting even weirder now. The BBC does not seem to be broadcasting! Flicking through all the other TV channels reveals nothing but static. You go upstairs and try another television unit, but with exactly the same result. Is your television aerial broken? What is going on?

You open your front door and notice that the bird song seems unusually loud. The normal buzz of human activity that would normally mask this so it is barely noticeable has completely vanished. You knock on your neighbour's door. No response. The same happens when you try the neighbour on the other side. Where is everyone? You try to phone your partner. No answer. You check Facebook. There are no new posts from when you logged on last night before you went to bed!

This is really starting to freak you out. With a sense of mounting panic you get in your car and cruise the streets to try to get a handle on what is going on. There is not a soul to be seen. Not in your village. Not on the motorway. Not in the local city.

Where is everyone? You don't know it yet, but after a few more days of this it will start to dawn on you that you might just be the last person on planet earth!

However this is not your typical Hollywood disaster movie; both you and planet earth are still in rude health. There has been no natural disaster or Armageddon. All the other humans have simply vanished never to return. Perhaps they have been transported to another dimension. The reason for this situation does not really matter. The fact is that you are now the king of the world. You own everything.

You can walk into an empty car showroom or jewellery store and help yourself. Whether it's a top of the range Ferrari, a Bentley or a rare vintage car, a Rolex watch or a pair of diamond encrusted Jimmy Choos, they are all yours for the taking. This is supermarket sweep without limitation. The stuff of dreams. All of the consumer goods on the planet are yours. You can take whatever you fancy! Need a change of scenery? Why don't you try a penthouse suite with a waterfront view?

When you get bored of that you can simply help yourself to the keys of a super yacht. Now you can experience a different view each day and watch the best that Mother Nature has to offer from the oceans and waterways of the world.

Yet in this altered context, most of the dream possessions in the world rapidly lose their former allure. With no one to see you wear that Armani suit or drive that Aston Martin, with no one to share that amazing sunset from the balcony of your apartment overlooking the river Thames, Lake Como, Sydney Harbour or Central Park, all of these treasures shine much less brightly.

Be Careful What You Wish For

It does not need to take an improbable mass exodus of the planet to make aspirational objects lose their allure. Remember the 27 club and all those other young A-listers who died prematurely. These people achieved fame and fortune. Some were musicians, others were film stars. They were all 'Rock Stars' in their own fields.

They were all wealthy. They had the means to buy the kind of material possessions that they had formally dreamed about. Yet their high octane drink and drug lifestyles which ultimately killed them highlight that this material wealth did not make them happy.

One of the problems of being a real Rock Star or celebrity is knowing who to trust. Knowing who likes you for being you, not just the kudos of being associated with a 'star.'

This is the reason that so many famous people either:

Marry someone who they knew before they became a celebrity
Or
Partner up with another celebrity who is already in the same boat and already has the same (or similar) status and wealth that they have.

Material wealth in the absence of meaningful human companionship is unfulfilling and the joy short lived.

What the Go-getters and the Humbles teach us

Shiny material things and status can be seductive. However, the enjoyment of new things tends to be relatively short-lived. People who allow materialism to become dominant in their search for happiness, constantly crave their next fix. Don't let obsession with what money can buy, blind you to the cost that earning the money carries. Successful Rock Star Retirees think and behave more like the Humbles by being mindful of price and cost in a more three-dimensional sense. They can see the relationship between money, quality time and relationships. This helps them to remain objective, to value the things that are really important and that will lead to happiness which is sustainable. Personally, my admiration for the Humbles as great parents far outweighs any of the material or status-related achievements of the Go-getters.

The perils of keeping up with the Joneses and the Go-getters

Achieving tangible wealth **and** enjoying happiness and quality time are not mutually exclusive. While it is totally possible for people to achieve both — during my life and career, I have seen plenty of examples — I do have to concede that people who achieve this are in the minority. This evidence suggested to me that it is easier to achieve a happier existence and a more fulfilling life if you turn down your consumerism button a few notches. On researching[26] this further, it's sad to see that the finding of a 2010 research paper, based on a sample of 10,000 people over a

---

[26]   Dr Chris Boyce, of University of Warwick's psychology department, in 2010

seven-year period, the researchers concluded that people were most happy when they had more than their neighbours.

"The standard of living has gone up for each individual over the past 40 years, but it has gone up for everyone. So our cars are faster now but our neighbours have faster cars too ... Without the biggest home, or the fastest car, then it doesn't give you that same excitement as it would have."

In other words many people seem to only be happy if they are doing better than their neighbours! And not just keeping up with the Joneses or the Go-getters, but bettering them. What kind of mindset is that? Today it is probably true to say that the definition of 'neighbours' in the Facebook era perhaps needs redefining to encompass our wider social networks. This is exactly what happened to the Go-getters. Their immediate neighbours were not necessarily doing better than them, but many of their new peers within their extended social network, were.

In my experience, the small number of people who have both significant material wealth **and** genuine quality time and happiness are the ones whose primary source of enjoyment and wellbeing does **not** come from their possession and status symbols, it comes from enjoying a reasonable amount of quality time shared with others of a like mind.

Early Peak Syndrome

There is one other trend that this case study illustrates. It is very much a **real** rock star trait, one that happens to top musicians and top athletes. It can also happen to ordinary, ambitious, career-minded people too, but **not** to Rock Star Retirees. It is a concept best described as early career 'peaking'. I know this concept all too well, because I witnessed it happen to my own father.

Although it is too early to see how things pan out for the Go-getters, I suspect that they have reached their career peaks too. Achieving significant success, status or even fame at a young age, is a mixed blessing. For most people who achieve this, the only way is sideways, or more likely down. A Premier League footballer, for example, can expect an average of eight years in the top flight. Although a handful each year go on to become television pundits or managers, the majority fall quickly away from the limelight of celebrity and their earning power sinks like a stone. Most footballers love the game, but when age catches up with them, this is taken away.

My own father was neither a rock star nor a sports star, but as a child, I thought he was even cooler! At the age of 18 he joined the British Royal Air Force and by 20, he was flying in jets as a navigator all around the world. He got to parachute into the sea, play war games with the Americans and hunt Russian submarines, as well as practice survival and evasion techniques while being pursued by the SAS. He was also involved with trials of early satellite navigation systems and was the last plane to leave the airstrip when Belize (British Honduras) was invaded. He was even featured in The Daily Telegraph when his plane landed safely after having a number of holes punched through it by a lightning storm. However, at the age of 40 after living this amazing life, he left the Royal Air Force and spent the next three years training for a new and a very different career but still on behalf of her Majesty. He became a tax inspector and went from flying fast jets to receiving insults, from the businessmen who had tried to navigate around the tax system, when he issued the news that they owed HMRC an awful lot more tax. To be fair to my father, his new work was actually pretty interesting and he went on to (and in retirement continues) to set himself exciting goals and projects and to live life to the full. However, based on how much he still talks about it, nothing has ever quite lived up to those amazing years of flying fast jets and being an English version of Top Gun! [27]

When life is rosy, enjoy it, but never take it for granted, savour every good bit. For all of us, our experience of life comes in peaks and troughs. However, allowing your career to overly define your sense of purpose, success or identity, without other facets to your life, can be a dangerous game. Rock Star Retirees ensure balance and mitigate risk by maintaining perspective of where they are and what is important, ensuring that they remember that the simple things in life can provide ample sources of stimulation, self-worth and meaning. This does not mean

[27] My dad's exploits are documented in Phil Keeble's book "Patrolling the Cold War Skies (Reheat Sunset)" published May 2017.

avoiding reaching for the sky, it is just about keeping perspective and enjoying and appreciating the good things in life, big or small.

"First I was dying to finish high school and go to college.
And then I was dying to finish college and start working.
And then I was dying to marry and have children.
And then I was dying for my children to
grow old enough for school so I could go back to work.
And then I was dying to retire.
And now I am dying …
and suddenly I realise I forgot to live"

ORIGINAL SOURCE UNKNOWN.

Heed these wise words, you are where you are today, but time is precious. Whatever your age and whatever your physical fitness, it is time to seize the day and make the most of the here and now, as well as the unprecedented opportunities our age has to offer.

LESSON 7 SUMMARY

Rock Star Retirement: Managing Your Career

As the parallel, yet very different paths of our case study couples [the Go-getters and the Humbles] illustrated very clearly, all that glitters is definitely not always gold.

The 'aspirational' lifestyle of a continuous upward trajectory on the career ladder in order to fuel a habit of financing 'big ticket' status symbol cars, houses and holidays is unlikely to be a path to happiness for most people.

Cash rich and time poor is not a great combination. Having a fancy job, a beautiful home, a flashy car, wonderful kids and the perfect partner sounds idyllic, but if you are always at work [physically, or mentally] then you won't ever really get to enjoy or appreciate the other riches you have.

For those that genuinely love their work, it pays to remember that career paths are pyramidal. There is **always** a ceiling. When you have gone as far as you are going to go, you are going to need other things in your life from which to derive satisfaction. Make sure that your kids have not grown up and left home, or that your partner has not divorced you before this realisation dawns!

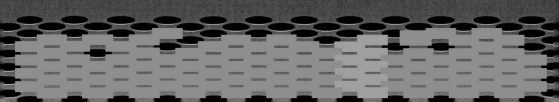

LESSON 8

WHAT SHOULD YOUR ROCK STAR RETIREMENT LOOK LIKE?

"It's a musical journey"

LARRY MULLEN JUNIOR, U2 — Rattle and Hum

Originally, when I released issue 1, the book cover was the image below. I chose it for a specific reason and I'm still very fond of it. I am pretty confident that looking at it, you will assume that the Rockstar Retiree was the older man? On first impression most readers perceive him to be a happily retired man filling his days with exciting adventures and one-off experiences; living the later stages of his life to the maximum.

Having now invested significant time in reading to this point, which of the 2 people do you *now* think is the Rock Star Retiree? By now, you are probably realising that it is just as likely to be the younger man; someone who has perhaps forgone a 5-day-a-week, 9–5 desk job and who is now getting paid to do something he loves, with the added benefit of getting to share his passion with other people.

The truth is that the image is the only example in the whole book that is not a real-life case study. It is simply a stock photograph that my editor Taryn picked out because it makes for a great visual metaphor for the whole Rock Star Retirement Concept. We chose this as the final image for the book jacket because we felt that **both** men were potential Rock Star Retirees. No surprises there for you by now, I hope.

My interpretation of the circumstances of these 2 men also went a step beyond this. As Rock Star Retirees, it is equally likely that **both** men still work in part-time, more conventional jobs elsewhere and that neither of them has actually retired in the conventional sense. After all, when you think about it, why would you bother to execute a traditional retirement 'escape' if you have got your work-life balance just right and are living and loving life on your own terms?

Going back to the book cover, one might suppose that the younger, professional skydiver loves the sensation of freefall with every fibre of his being; he just can't get enough of testing and playing chicken with Newton's laws! At the same time, it is very possible that the older man, although smiling for the camera, is actually feeling horribly sick as he plummets perilously towards the earth with his body uncomfortably close to a complete stranger wearing a dodgy Elvis jumpsuit.

When he finally has his feet safely back on terra firma, has unhooked, regained his personal space and had sufficient time for the adrenaline to wear off, he will probably thank his lucky stars that he survived, feel satisfied that he can now tick skydiving off his bucket list, and will vow firmly never to repeat the experience again! Both men are Rock Star Retirees, both shared a common activity, yet their experience and enjoyment of the event were poles apart.

The point is that one person's ideal Rock Star Retirement may be another's nightmare. How we enjoy to spend our precious time is just as subjective as our taste in music. Perhaps the younger guy likes Heavy Metal and the older man Mozart. Or it could be the other way around; as my dear old Mum likes to say, never judge a book by its cover and never judge a man by his jumpsuit! (Okay, I made the second bit up!).

The aim is that to enable us to plan and shape our own unique Rock Star Retirement path, we must first delve deeper into the question of **why we need to retire at all.** I have considered this question intensely for nearly 2 decades and have observed that the need or desire to retire, in a conventional sense, appears to stem from 3 main things:

1. A person suffers a deterioration of health, physical or mental, that prevents them from doing their job safely or effectively.

2. The time a person is committing to their work is preventing them from doing other activities that they have a strong desire to experience or achieve within their lifetime. As people get older, they get an increasing sense and realisation that time is finite, and this leads to a major rethink and restructure of how they are going to live their life going forward.

3. A person detests the reality of their working life so much that they are desperate to escape as soon as practically possible. The reasons that people find themselves in this position can be very varied and are numerous and we will explore this further in a moment.

Exercise:

Q: Do any of these 3 reasons why people actively seek to retire apply to you right now?

A: _____

Q: Could any of these 3 reasons why people retire apply to you in the future and if so which one is the most likely cause and on what timescale?

A: _____

Let's drill down a little deeper by looking at each retirement catalyst in turn and by asking a few key questions to help us understand them better. This will enable us to see where and how we might shape things in our favour. I have also added in a 4th catalyst to change too — a positive one.

Reason for retirement:
Reaching financial goals/critical mass that means a person no longer needs to go to work to pay for a reasonable lifestyle.

Desirable: Yes!

Likelihood of affecting you/likelihood of achievement?
Fully achievable, if you set clear goals and priorities and follow the right strategy.

Can be influenced?
Yes! The key is via the choices you make. These are very personal. It is you who ultimately decides how much you earn, spend and save, how life is lived, what day-to-day and future living costs are.

Reason for retirement:
A person suffers a deterioration of health, physical or mental, that prevents them from doing their job safely or effectively.

Desirable: No!

Likelihood of affecting you/likelihood of achievement?
As we saw in the Rock Star Ageing Lesson, this is 100% guaranteed to afflict all of us at some point; at least until scientists find a way to stop the ageing process, or archaeologists find the mystical fountain of youth (my money is on the scientists, but probably not in my or your lifetime).

Can be influenced?
For most of us, yes! As we explored in the Rock Star health and ageing lessons, living a balanced, clean life improves the chances of us ducking any major health issues until much later in life and boosts our chances of remaining active for much longer.

Reason for retirement:
Person feels that by working, they are missing out on other life goals—and that their life clock is ticking!

Desirable: No!

Likelihood of affecting you/likelihood of achievement?
Yes, if you passively follow the conventional life plan and traditional approach to retirement.
For example, if one of your dreams is to get your golf handicap down to 10 and you are now 55, if you leave it much longer, this is going to become harder and harder to achieve.

Can be influenced?
Yes! In most cases you can renegotiate your terms of work, or your finances to allow the desired itch to be scratched. You might be able to work 4 days a week instead of 5, perhaps "buying" yourself two extra workday afternoons to get out on the golf course. This might mean a reduction in money, but a pay rise in terms of quality time and life experience.

Reason for retirement:
Detest job and/or career and passionately seek a complete exit/retirement as soon as financially practical.

Desirable: No!

Likelihood of affecting you/likelihood of achievement?
Depends upon your chosen career and specialism, your working environment, colleagues, clients, workplace culture and your attitude towards change and lifelong learning. The workplace and the modern world are evolving at an unprecedented speed.
If you are not adaptive in your thinking and are not prepared to learn new skills, then it is very likely that you will fall out of love with your job, your employer, colleagues, staff, or customers will fall out of love with you.

Can be influenced?

Yes! The power for change is in your own hands. This may require an external change such as a move to a different, more fulfilling role, or a transfer to a different company with a more positive culture. Alternatively, it may require an internal change, a change of attitude or direction etc.

As you can see, ALL of the main reasons that people seek to retire can, for most people, be proactively and positively influenced to allow them to be either deferred to a later date, or in some instances, be completely removed.

Now let me ask a theoretical question. If all 3 of the **negative** reasons that motivate people to seek retirement were absent, would people ever want to fully retire? Take a look at the table below to see what this scenario might look like.

What happens when we remove the normal drivers for retirement?

Normal reason for retirement	Opposite position
A deterioration of health, strength or senses, making it no longer possible to perform job/ career role any longer to a satisfactory, or safe, standard.	You are in good health for your age and there is no sign of age being a barrier to you being able to do your job really well. On the contrary, compared to many of your peers, you feel like the fact that you keep busy and stimulated at work keeps you sharper and younger. You don't need to work, but you choose to work, so it is all now on your own terms.

Normal reason for retirement	Opposite position
Feeling that by working, you are missing out on other life goals, and the clock is ticking!	You are happily and methodically working your way through your bucket list month, by month, year by year. With the kids safely graduated from university and living fully independent lives now and the mortgage paid off, the extra revenue from continuing to work allows you afford amazing and exotic holidays every year — something that the annuity from your pension would not. I have a client in his mid-30s who owns an optical practice. He persuaded his staff to work 10 hours per day in return for an extra day off. They work hard during the 4 working days and all now have a 3-day weekend. This enables him to tick off more European city breaks from his bucket list each year.
Detest job or career and passionately seek an exit.	You find your job highly rewarding and stimulating.

None of us can cheat Father Time for ever (not even by drinking copious quantities of POM wonderful pomegranate juice as outlined on page 29), but all of us can aspire to live and enjoy a fulfilling life for longer — and to front load more fun on a day-to-day and year-to-year basis. So let's look at how to plan for this.

ANOTHER ROCK STAR WARNING! HEAVY CONTENT AHEAD!

Moving from living to work to working to live

There are 3 'mainstream' ways that people plan the transition from their working lives to their retired lives:

★ **The Ostrich approach** — advocates of this philosophy studiously ignore retirement planning in any shape or form. This "ignorance is bliss" philosophy arises from a belief that it is impossible and impractical to save enough to retire via traditional means, so why bother to plan. This strategy assumes that a person will simply work until they drop and relies on the value locked into their home, or the state or other people's charity (often family) to provide the subsistence and life-support when they can no longer work or support themselves.[28]

★ **The 'Big Bang' approach** — this is the typical solution advocated by financial advisers and the pension planning industry. It normally involves a dramatic watershed moment, when a person transitions from a life of full time work to a life of no work at all. The timing is normally (in theory) based upon hitting a specific pension pot amount or a milestone age (such as 65+.)

★ **A Phased approach** — a gradual cutting down of working hours to explore other pursuits, while continuing to work part-time, allowing for adaptation of lifestyle and in many cases, meaning that someone ends up working for longer, but with the quid pro quo that they free up more time at a younger age while their health is still good and choosing to do work that is still enjoyable in the later years.

---

[28] This is a reversion to the pre-retirement days of old as highlighted in lesson 1, when there was no such thing as retirement.

Perils of the Ostrich approach

Of the 3 approaches to retirement planning, the ostrich approach is by far the worst route to take. Relying on luck and the goodwill or charity of others and shirking personal responsibility is never a good thing. Expecting the state, or worse your children to house, feed or nurse you in your later years because you were too passive to face up to the issue and make some provision for yourself is bordering on the criminal. Thankfully I know that this does not apply to you because people with ostrich tendencies do not proactively seek out and read books on lifestyle and retirement planning! If you have only just taken your head out of the sand, then don't worry, there is still time to make a difference.

Big Bang theory flaws

As already highlighted in the detailed review of traditional retirement planning in the introduction, the problem with working flat out to hit a specific target (age and/or pension pot value) is that there are too many external variables and in far too many cases, a person's health declines prior to, or shortly after reaching their target. This means that they never have the good health to truly enjoy the fruits of their overly long-term delayed gratification strategy. And even where health is not an issue, the anecdotal evidence I have gathered, suggests that people who have worked long and hard in their professional careers and those who have run their own businesses, frequently struggle badly to adapt to the world outside the workplace in the aftermath of a big bang retirement.

As a consequence, I have seen:

★ Depression
★ The breakdown of relationships/divorce
★ A rapid deterioration in health, or sometimes even sudden death within months of retiring (many medical studies have reported that a reasonable level of day-to-day 'stress' is actually good for the human immune system).
★ People coming back to me to try and re-buy their old business, or another to replace the structure and busyness of their old lives

A Phased Approach

While everyone is different, in my experience, by far the happiest group are the last group, the people who opt for a more gradual, phased reduction of work.

Benefits of a phased retirement include:

★ More time to get used to life outside of the workplace.
★ The retention of relationships with colleagues in the workplace, while affording more opportunities to find new, or deepen, existing relationships in the wider world outside of work.
★ A great balance between having more free time to enjoy life, while still retaining a reasonable income (time richer and relatively cash rich).
★ A greater feeling of personal control. By proactively reducing their number of working days, people undertaking a phased retirement, experience a feeling of emancipation. They define it as a feeling that their job, boss or company now 'own' less of them and that the balance of power has shifted in their favour. Another positive, common side effect is that the scarcity of their time makes their employer, colleagues or customers actually value and appreciate them more.
★ The success and happiness of people retiring correlates strongly with them having, or developing, interests outside of work. A phased retirement approach is the ideal structure from which to develop new and rewarding ways to spend your time.

Bearing all of this in mind, for most people it is wrong to view 'retirement' as a **single phase** of your life. For those who start in good health, there are frequently a number of phases to retirement. It pays to understand this, so that you can plan and pace your goals and finances appropriately.

Phases of retirement can include:

Early days: Get the balance right, subject to a degree of luck in the life-health lottery, these can be very happy years, offering a period featuring a unique combination of ready access to the triple riches of being:

* Time rich
* Cash rich, perhaps from a pension lump sum or savings, possibly boosted by some form of enjoyable and carefully selected part-time work.
* Healthy enough to enjoy the other 2 'riches.'[29]

The 'early days' retirement phase represents the retirement dream that financial advisers promote, but one too few people who sign up to the programme actually ever truly achieve because of the reliance on the big bang, big target, approach.

Going for a phased retirement can allow you to hedge your health bets by allowing access to some of your savings and more quality time at an earlier stage.

Mid-days: getting older and slowing down. Still able to live independently, but less likely to want to spend money on 'big ticket items' such as fancy fast cars or expensive holidays involving long-haul travel. Annual financial requirements are likely to be more modest during the mid-retirement phase.

Final days: Although death is actually very rock and roll, we don't really want to dwell on this point! For completeness though, I do have to mention the fact that age really does catch up with us all at some point. Illness or a decline in physical or mental condition can get to a point prior to "the end of your days" when you are not capable of enjoying a normal quality of life any-more. As Benjamin Franklin famously said: "*In this world, nothing can be certain, except death and taxes.*" Ironically the 'cost' of this final phase of life can go up for some people, as they require expensive medical and care assistance just to get through each day.

As ever, it is not what life throws at us that counts, it is how we react to it. In this case, rather than dwell on it in a negative way, the fact that we age and ultimately die can be used in a positive way to make sure that we

---

[29] Multi-millionaire, former Formula One racing driver Michael Schumacher suffered a major head injury while skiing in 2014, providing a stark reminder of the fact that the pleasure that time and monetary wealth can bring are greatly diminished in the absence of good health.

seize the day earlier, making a plan that enables us to sensibly enjoy the good years when our health allows us to do so.

Jobs to die for (and to die in!)

Of course, there are always exceptions to the rule. Here are some enviable examples of people doing jobs to die for and to die in that I have picked up on my recent travels:[30]

★ Bruce, the guide who took my son and I, as well as the rest of our party, safely to the top of the Sydney Harbour Bridge. The summit is a specular 134 m above the harbour below, with panoramic views of what is arguably the most beautiful city on the planet, Bruce has quite an *office*. His working life includes different weather and wind conditions each day and the occasional celebrity to escort (famous bridge climbers have included the fastest man on earth, Usain Bolt, movie star Ben Stiller, TV star Oprah Whinfrey and rock star, David Hasselhof (look it up, he really is a rock star in Germany, as well as an American TV star!) Combine the social aspect, the vista and a passion for the history of the bridge build in 1923 and this is some job. Not a job to give up lightly!

★ Leon[31]– an amazingly charismatic guide who gave my family a personal tour[32] of Sydney's Taronga zoo, with an Aboriginal take on the importance of living in harmony and balance with nature. His fascination with native Australian plants and animals, his acting background, the beautiful environment and an all access pass makes his job seem more like play. Why on earth would he want to retire?

★ Karl, the marine biologist who took us out on a snorkelling tour of the Agincourt 2 reef in Australia, part of the outer Great Barrier

---

[30] They also highlight the fact that I am not writing this book as some sort of abstract theory, I am applying the Rock Star Retirement philosophy in my own life in my mid 40s.

[31] Leon Burchill is an Aboriginal musician, historian and actor — you can find out more about him via Wikipidia.

[32] The Nura Diya tour is highly recommended.

Reef. For a marine biologist with a passion for his subject, this has to be the world's biggest and most beautiful playground. With his job mostly based in the water, taking all of the weight off his joints and with the availability of flotation aids to make the snorkelling even easier, this is a job he could quite happily do until he was 80. Let's just hope the Great Barrier Reef survives that long, but that is another story for another book.

★ The guide who took my son and I out to witness the incredible spectacle of the Northern Lights in a beautiful forest in Finland. This incredible phenomenon lies way outside of my writing skills, but it is not a sight you could ever get bored of. I am told that no night is ever the same. And even when the Northern Lights don't show up, the lack of light pollution makes the clear northern Finnish night sky an incredible stargazing experience in its own right, with the freshest air you could ever breathe. Apart from the unsociable hours, this is another dream job and not one to trade in for days in front of the TV, as long as your legs still work.

★ The pilot of a light aircraft in New Zealand who flew us over some of the landscapes featured as the Misty Mountains in Lord of The Rings and The Hobbit and then into the amazing fiord, Milford Sound. Likewise, also in New Zealand, the helicopter pilot who flew us past Mount Cook and landed us on a glacier.

★ Our guide and trained naturalist and historian who escorted my friends and I when we trekked the Inca Trail to Machu Pichu, Peru and then the Amazon rainforest.

With these kind of jobs, there is a blurring between work and play, very genuine 'Rock Star' traits. No doubt by now, you will have figured out that real life 'Rock Stars' never actually retire. They love what they do, and they keep on rocking until the very end, or until they can no longer hold a guitar, microphone or drum stick.

TOP 5 'ROCK STAR' ON STAGE DEATHS AND POST-PERFORMANCE "PASSINGS"

1. **Johnny "Guitar" Watson**, American blues, soul and funk musician who died aged 61 in 1996 from a heart attack while performing on stage in Japan.

2. **Mark Sandman**, multi-talented US-born, singer songwriter and musician, know best as the base guitarist and lead vocalist of the Canadian band, Morphine. He died on stage of a heart attack while performing in Italy in 1999, aged 46.

3. **Tommy Cooper**, British magician and comedian. In 1984, aged 63, he suffered a fatal heart attack while performing live on UK national television. People initially thought his collapse on stage was part of his comedy act.

4. **Eric Morecambe**, comedian and half of the British national comedy treasure duo Morecambe and Wise. He suffered a fatal heart attack in 1984, aged 58, as he left the stage having performed in a charity event in Cheltenham.

5. **Carrie Fisher**, actress synonymous with her role as Star Wars' Princess Leia. She stopped breathing while flying home to the US after appearing on The Graham Norton show in London, shortly after completing filming of Star Wars, The Last Jedi. She died 4 days later aged 60.

In the same way, many of the jobs to die in or die for require modest physical ability, therefore age to some extent is a boon rather than a drawback, "with age comes experience"[33] and wisdom and age brings more stories, more knowledge, more experience.

All of these jobs to die for, and to die in, feature nature, or a beautiful, dynamic, epic environment of some description. I am not suggesting that you up sticks and relocate, although there are worse things you can do. These are just examples of jobs I have admired over recent years which appeal to me. Your tastes and dreams may be completely different. However, it is important to be objective and remember that despite being in their dream job, these lucky people will have good days and bad days at 'the office,' but I suspect many more exceptionally good days than the average employee.

Question: Is there a dream job out there for your Rock Star Retirement?

Answer: _____

Question: What would you have to do to get the role?

Answer: _____

Question: When could you start?

Answer: _____

The elephant in the room when answering the last question is, of course, the small matter of money. Don't worry, we will deal with that in the next lesson. For now, let's park this practical detail to give us full scope for some blue sky thinking about what your Rock Star retirement could look like.

---

[33] This expression now always reminds me of Johnny English Reborn, one of my son's favourite films and one for your film bucket list if you have not yet seen it!

To get the most out of your life and retirement you need to make sure that your precious time is filled with things that make **you** feel fulfilled and happy. This is one of the only times when I will recommend that you do dwell on the past, however, not in a state of dewy-eyed, nostalgia with a *"didn't it used to be great back then"* attitude. Moreover, you need to spend time looking at your past with a keen eye on shaping your future.

What happened in the past cannot be changed or undone. What you need to look for are patterns. Patterns in terms of what is it that **really makes you happy?**

Exercise

Think back over your life so far. Take a couple of minutes to jot down the 10 or 20 most memorable positive things to date:

1. _____

2. _____

3. _____

4. _____

5. _____

6. _____

7. _____

8. _____

9. _____

10. _____

11. _____

12. _____

13. _____

14. _____

15. _____

16. _____

17. _____

18. _____

19. _____

20. _____

To get the most out of this book, you do need to invest the time to complete the exercises, so please don't just read on regardless. This exercise will only take a few minutes and, apart from being helpful, most people also find the experience of putting pen to paper on their life's highlights extremely uplifting and therapeutic. Invest some quality me time in thought and reflection.

Most people's answers are likely to include a few the following:

★ Meeting your life partner
★ Your wedding
★ The birth of your children
★ A success from your formative years which might be winning a race at school or perhaps an award or acknowledgement
★ One or more stand out holidays or travel experiences
★ A "perfect day"
★ A memorable night out
★ A stand out concert, theatre production or sporting event
★ Watching a favourite film or listening to a particular piece of music or album
★ Reading a favourite book or watching a favourite TV show
★ Your 15 minutes of fame …
★ Your children's wedding(s)
★ Buying your first house
★ The birth of your grandchildren
★ Encounters with famous people …

Your answers will also almost certainly fit in with this common theme; the vast majority of our happiest memories come from **experiences** rather than physical **material possessions**.

Now that is quite enough navel-gazing and retrospection. It is time to look forward with optimism and excitement. It is time to begin to hatch a plan!

As a Rock Star Retiree, you are going to have less time working and more discretionary time. Having identified the types of things that make you feel fulfilled and leave a lasting memory, it is time to identify more of these things that truly make you happy, that you want to do in the future.

Exercise

Write down the first 10–20 things that you desire to do going forward, these may range from big ticket dream holidays to simple relationship goals such as spending more quality time with friends and family. Write down the first 20 things that pop into your head. There are no right or wrong answers. Don't spend too long initially trying to produce a perfect all-encompassing document. It is not a fixed list, just a starting point.

1. _____

2. _____

3. _____

4. _____

5. _____

6. _____

7. _____

8. _____

9. _____

10. _____

11. _____

12. _____

13. _____

14. _____

15. _____

16. _____

17. _____

18. _____

19. _____

20. _____

From experience, your initial list is likely to be a mixture of different, mainly random ideas. There may also be groupings of associated themes, such as places to visit.

A Rock Star Retiree's list is very much a dynamic thing. Long term, this will ideally be an electronic document that you can add to, tick off and restructure as your priorities and means change and as you proceed through life. I can guarantee that there are things out there that you will want to do that you have not even thought about yet.

Let's end this lesson with something for you to consider:

Question; Are there any items on your "activities to do" list created in the previous exercise that you could do right away?

Answer: _____

_____

_____

Question: Are there any activities on your to do list that you could do in the next 12 months?

Answer: _____

_____

_____

Question: With the exclusion of 'big ticket' items with cost/budgetary constraints, why have you not done them and what is stopping you?

Answer: _____

_____

_____

Question: Is there something you could change in your life over the next 12 months to overcome this blockage?

Answer: _____

_____

_____

Again, don't worry too much about the detail for now, these questions are just to get you to begin to think.

ROCK STAR RETIREMENT
HUMOUR

What are the 3 main reasons that ageing Rock Stars decide to retire?

1. They forgot the lyrics to "Oo-Oo, Oo-Oo."

2. When they played power chords, it was causing horrible hearing-aid feedback.

3. They became tired of illicit drug addiction and were ready to start on prescription drug addiction.

Please forward any complaints about the poor quality of these jokes directly to their source which was www.grinningplanet.com !

LESSON 8 SUMMARY

(what should Your Rock Star Retirement look like?)

As the photograph on the front cover illustrates, Rock Star Retirees come from all ages and backgrounds. Individual preferences and tastes mean that one person's dream retirement lifestyle can be very different from anothers.

What is desirable during one phase of your retirement is also likely to evolve as you age and this needs to be factored into your planning to allow for a degree of flexibility.

There are 3 main reasons why people desire to retire:

★ Illness/ageing makes it impossible or uncomfortable to carry out the work in a safe, satisfactory or enjoyable manner.

★ Getting older brings home the fact that time is finite and that their time spent working prevents them from doing other things they are keen to do during their lifetime.

★ A person hates their job so much that they are desperate to escape.

It is possible to proactively influence all 3, to reduce or at least delay, the desire to retire in the conventional sense:

★ Living a sustainable, healthy lifestyle increases the chances of avoiding major illnesses and premature ageing, increasing the ability of a person to work and be active for longer.

★ It is possible to change your work patterns and hours to allow you to do more leisure activities at an earlier age, for example, negotiating more holidays, or perhaps reducing your working days to allow you to do some of the things you were planning to do during a conventional retirement, much earlier whilst your health is good.

★ If you genuinely detest your job, the situation is totally in your own hands. You have the power to do something positive about it. This can be scary, but surely so is the prospect of hating and wasting the rest of your working life?

Some people work full time until they drop. However, for the majority of people, following conventional retirement planning strategies, there are 3 options when planning the transition from working life to retirement:

1. The **Ostrich** approach — ignore the subject completely and hope for the best.

2. The **'Big Bang'** approach — target a specific milestone or pension pot saving sum and work flat out full time until it is reached.

3. A **Phased** approach — a graduated reduction in working days to enable a gentle transition.

On the whole, the happiest group are the people who go for a phased approach.

When thinking through your retirement strategy, it pays to factor in, that for most people, retirement is not a single phase. Phases can include:

1. **Early days** — in good health and potentially able to enjoy life and the newfound quality time extensively.

2. **Mid-days** — in less robust health, but still able to enjoy life, just not such an active one.

3. **End of days** — in poor health, severely compromised health leading to a very poor life quality with a high dependency on care from other people.

Each person's journey is different, and some people may miss out on one or more of the stages completely. However, traditional pension and financial planning means that far too many people miss out phase 1 altogether. Don't let this be you.

There are a number of jobs available that blur the boundaries between work and play. I refer to them as "jobs to die for and die in." Can you identify a job like this for your Rock Star Retirement?

When we reflect on our lives so far, the majority of the most memorable events are experiences, rather than 'things'.

In planning our futures, it makes sense to shoot for more of the same kinds of things that have been memorable and have provided long-lasting enjoyment and fulfilment.

Are there any items on your 'to do' list that you could do immediately or perhaps within the next 12 months? Other than expensive big-ticket items, such as a trip to Australia, consider and carefully think about what is holding you back? Is there something you could change to make this happen?

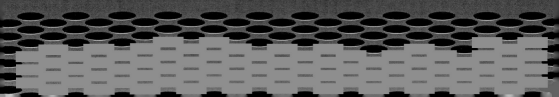

LESSON 9

FUNDING YOUR ROCK STAR RETIREMENT

YOUR JOURNEY TO A FASTER RETIREMENT

But you can keep them for the birds and bees
Now give me money, That's what I want,
That's what I want, yeah, That's what I want
You're lovin' gives me a thrill
But you're lovin' don't pay my bills
Now give me money, That's what I want,
That's what I want, yeah, That's what I want
Money don't get everything it's true
What it don't get, I can't use
Now give me money, That's what I want,
That's what I want, yeah, That's what I want, wah
Money don't get everything it's true
What it don't get, I can't use
Now give me money, That's what I want,
That's what I want, yeah
That's…

MONEY (THAT'S WHAT I WANT)—Barrett Strong (1959)

Legal Disclaimer

The author is NOT qualified to provide financial advice. The content of this chapter is therefore written solely with the intention of being thought-provoking. It is NOT written as practical advice on how to plan your retirement finances.

We are legally obliged to recommend that you seek advice from a professional financial adviser with the relevant qualifications. However, we do not recommend that you follow the mainstream advice they will initially seek to give you. Instead, why not get them to formally work through some of the ideas and strategies provided here, to give you the best of both worlds.

Advisory Note:

Whoa! 2 disclaimers at the start of a single chapter. This has to set some kind of new record! I have kept the tone light, but Lesson 9 is a crucial section of the book. As the subtitle suggests, this lesson is going to take you on something of a journey. Like some of the previous content, the initial propositions may appear abstract when you read them for the first time. All I ask, is that you stick with it and don't draw any firm conclusions until you have read the WHOLE of the lesson and are in possession of the full message.

RADICAL RETIREMENT PLANS

Based on the mainstream life plan, set out by your bank or financial adviser, how far off is the day that you will be in a strong enough financial position to afford to retire? 5 years? A decade? 20 years? Even longer? If you were previously a member of the Ostrich retirement planning fraternity, perhaps never?

Empowered by the knowledge that there are alternative retirement pathways and strategies available to you, it is now time to consider how much quicker you can get to where you want to be.

Think very carefully before you settle on an answer to the following question:

If you were prepared to make drastic changes to your life such as reducing spending, boosting savings and became truly committed to a single-minded pursuit. How much earlier do you believe you could reach your retirement objectives? 2 years? 5 Years? Perhaps even a decade.

Operation Immediate Retirement

What if I told you that you could execute a plan right away that would allow you to retire immediately? Yes, you read that correctly, immediately! No delay; No need for further saving! Sounds implausible doesn't it, but if your current life motivates you to such an extent that you are prepared to take drastic action, then this is genuinely achievable for most people. Let me explain how by starting with some basic facts.

A study in 2014 determined that in the event of a total sale of all of their assets, the average British adult has a total realizable net worth of £147,134.[34]

Exercise

Read the definition below and then work out your own approximate net worth figure.

My net worth is £ _____

ROCK STAR RETIREMENT TIP:

The study defined personal assets as: property equity, savings, investments, pensions, cars and possessions. These are the assets that you need to tot up, minus any outstanding debts you would need to pay off. So, for clarity, Operation Immediate Retirement does NOT involve THAT kind of operation; there is no need to sell off any of your truly personal assets, such as one of your kidneys[35] (phew), or your mother-in-law (sorry) to achieve this figure, just your material possessions.

---

[34] Daily Mail article, 5 March 2014.

[35] Joking aside, for those intrigued by this subject, Google the article *"Which Organs Can I Live Without, and How Much Cash Can I Get for Them?"* If this does not give you some perspective on your life, and the desperate measures some people have to make to survive, or raise money to care for their loved ones, then nothing will.

Mother-in-law jokes aside, how did you get on and how do your finances currently stack up? Is your net worth figure higher or lower than the UK average?

Unsurprisingly, our personal value tends to increase with age. Having had less time working, earning and saving, people in their 20s or 30s are naturally likely to be worth less than people in their 40s or 50s.

For people whose assets meet, or exceed the £147,134 average UK level, I have stunning news for you. You are in a position **right now** to hand in your notice and quit your job, confident that you have the means to cease working and live off the proceeds for pretty much the rest of your life.

Did your financial adviser tell you that you needed a much larger pension pot, or that you had to work for another decade or two? Did the financial planning calculator tool you used online — the one with two dozen disclaimers about its accuracy — tell you that you needed to save more and work for longer? Of course they did!

Don't worry, all will be explained in a minute, but first, let's give some hope to those whose current asset value does not yet meet this average figure? Based on the same concept, even from a standing start, with hard work and a little sacrifice you could probably build up enough savings in a 10–15 year timescale to permanently retire too. Even more encouragingly, whatever the value of your current assets, you can almost certainly **semi-retire immediately,** by working part time and still afford a great standard of life!

So, what is the secret of super early retirement and where did you find it?

Most significant discoveries come to us via some form of journey. It is only in taking ourselves out of our bubble, our normal, limited window on the world, that truth and reality are revealed, providing a proper context on our lives and belief systems. Such discoveries are best told within the framework of the journey itself, so here is the story of how at the age of 43, I realised that I was **already** in a position to retire from the world of work — and the fact that other people of similar 'average' means could do so too — if we are prepared to change our thinking and lifestyle.

An East African epiphany

It was in Ethiopia in November 2015 that this early retirement revelation came to me. My generation's perception of Ethiopia originates from the harrowing, vivid footage of emaciated children and grieving mothers that epitomised the terrible famine of 1984. In their quest to raise awareness and aid, pop stars Bob Geldof, Bono, Bowie and their Band Aid brothers left a disturbing, lasting impression. As a result, I had envisaged a hot, dry, dusty and desperately poor place and downtrodden, broken people. But my reference point on Ethiopia is an outdated one and 'my lens' on this country was gravely distorted, because the current reality is entirely different.

The drought and famine from the "Feed the world" music video are long gone. These days Ethiopia has a surprisingly lush, green and fertile landscape. It is also no second-rate rural backwater. The capital Addis Ababa is home to the African League of Nations,[36] making it the political centre of Africa. Underpinned by political stability[37] the economy is expanding in excess of 10% a year, making it not only the fastest growing African economy, but also the third fastest growing economy in the world.[38] Definitely a country on the up and a very different place from most Westerners' perceptions.

Whilst, advancements have been huge, the development of the country is very much still a work in progress. Inequality is still rife, poverty widespread and infrastructure basic, but for those with even relatively modest means (by Western standards) there is an opportunity to have an amazing lifestyle there.

---

[36]   Similar to Brussels being the political heart of the European Union.

[37]   By African standards!

[38]   "The 5 Fastest Growing Countries in the World" published by the Motley Fool, November 2014.

For example, the tap water in the capital is drinkable and the hotel I stayed in had both high-speed broadband and cable television (and as you will see in a minute, it was not a big brand 5 star chain hotel). I was even able to watch my football team, Manchester United beat Watford live on the TV in my room during a 3pm GMT Saturday kick off, something I would never get to do back home in England.

It may seem an unconventional and radical change but with the average UK adult's realizable £147,000 (a small fortune), a new start in Ethiopia could be quite grand. Labour costs across the country are incredibly low, therefore you could hire a maid or a gardener to help grow your own bananas. Imagine sitting back sipping a local Tomoca Coffee or St. George beer.

It won't be all plain sailing of course. There would be sacrifices to be made and things that you would miss. Whilst brands such as Coca Cola seem to be available in even the most remote areas, many products and consumer items that we take for granted are not readily available in Ethiopia.

Additionally to this, time in Africa seems to be more 'relative', especially in Ethiopia who use their own 13-month calendar. Therefore during my visit in 2015, it was considered to be 2008 in Ethiopia. If you were to retire here then you would certainly be time rich! Finally, Medical facilities are basic but for those with a little money, private healthcare is available in the main populated areas.

While in Ethiopia, I was fortunate to take part in an incredible personal journey. I hope that you will forgive a little reminiscing and the opportunity to share my trip report with you. I hope that it will help to inspire and motivate you to go on your own personal voyage of discovery, to follow your dreams and to write your own story.

Vision Aid/Great Ethiopian Run Trip Report 2015

Unless your name is Mo, it is never a good idea to race an Ethiopian, especially in their own backyard. Yet that is exactly what 36 of us set out to do when we took part in the high altitude Great Ethiopian Run in

Addis Ababa to raise funds for the charity Vision Aid Overseas (VAO). Our party was an eclectic mix of VAO hierarchy, clinical professionals, optical practice staff and back office support staff. There were also representatives working in the broader optical industry and a few people from outside of optics simply looking to raise money for a great cause and to share this unique experience.

The first day was mostly dedicated to travel, and settling into our base, the hilariously named, but surprisingly comfortable, Caravan Hotel. After an initial briefing, we went out for a meal and began the process of getting to know each other (AKA sizing up the 'competition'). Who worked for an independent, a multiple[39] or other optical company, who was a serious runner, jogger or walker? We truly were a diverse mix, but from the word go, it was clear that we were all going to get along.

After a fitful first night's sleep, we headed for the GTM project Butajira. This involved a bumpy 4-hour drive south of our base in Addis Ababa. However, the dust, heat and discomfort were more than made up for by

---

[39] Who owned/works for an optical chain or franchise such as Vision Express, Boots Opticians or Specsavers.

some stunning scenery in what is a surprisingly green and fertile country.

The GTM[40] project is a medical centre encompassing eye care and eyewear services managed by Vision Aid Overseas, as well as offering other services ranging from the treatment of epilepsy through to audiology.

We were given a warm and informative guided tour and treated to some excellent Ethiopian food and a very special 'coffee ceremony.' It was a wonderful, humbling experience to get proper boots on the ground and to see the benefits to the local population of VAO's work. This was the fundamental reason for our trip, our fundraising would support this and other similar projects in Ethiopia and beyond.

The next day was spent touring the sights of Addis together. Highlights included a visit to the National Museum to see "Lucy" the skeleton of the world's oldest known hominoid, (surprisingly short), a Tomaca coffee shop (the best coffee I have ever tasted) and magnificent views of Addis from mount Entoto (a lung-burning 3 times the height of Snowdon!)

On the eve of the race, we were treated to a pasta party at the Hilton Addis. Some of the more serious runners stuck to disciplined hydration regimes. The rest of us enjoyed the superb food, music and dancing accompanied by generous quantities of the excellent local St George's beer. To round off an incredible evening, we got to meet and have our pictures taken with double Olympic champion Haile Gebrselassie. There are some things that money just can't buy. What a spectacular honour to meet this legend before sharing his final ever race.

Finally, it was time to line up on race day. Serious athlete or fun runner, Ethiopian or westerner, rich or poor, we all wore the same race T-shirt and were caught up in the pre-race euphoria. The atmosphere was more akin to a carnival than a sporting event. As we waited for the race to begin, we sang, partied, danced, took photographs and mixed with our fellow runners. The atmosphere was electric and emotional, a sponta-

---

[40] GTM stands for Grarbet Tehadiso Mahber (project)

neous outpouring of joy and solidarity, totally at odds with the normal doom and gloom stories about a divided world in conflict as reported daily by our media. Then we were off, a teaming singing wave of joyous humanity washing through the streets of Addis. Having suffered a double hernia in training, I was never going to set any course records, I was just grateful to be taking part and enjoyed just being able take it all in.

The course was hilly, the heat and the altitude draining. There were potholes that could have doubled as tank traps and the stench when we ran through the cattle market was as caustic as mustard gas. Yet these perils made the event more memorable and were offset by the sheer joyous chaos of it all. We were frequently forced to slow down to a slow jog or a brisk walk as fellow runners obstructed the way ahead as they stopped to dance to one of the many bands or to take a quick beer on board as we passed a cafe. All too soon, my slowest ever 10k by some distance was over and I had a medal around my neck.

Tired but elated, we headed back to the Caravan (hotel!) to freshen up for a post-race party held by GTM. Time for more music, dancing, food and drink and a chance to swap stories about our individual experiences of the race.

For those of us who had not been to Africa before, we came home changed. For all of us, it was a great context check and a chance to make many new, strong friendships and memories forged in the heat of the African sun and likely to last a lifetime.

I have been lucky enough to have run marathons, hiked the Great Wall of China, walked the Inca Trail and swum with dolphins in New Zealand, yet for me this is one event and one overall experience that stands above all others as a multi-sensory, fulfilling, memorable and meaningful trip. As I have eulogised about my experience, people have subsequently asked me how I am going to ever follow it up, the only thing I can think of is to do it all again and next time, to take my children to run with me to share the experience too.

This liberating, eye-opening experience epitomises what a Rock Star Retirement can be. Not only was I able to work and do good for others, but I was also able to experience something that was completely off the scale when it came to a 9–5 existence.

I am not for one minute suggesting that Ethiopia is the perfect retirement destination or lifestyle choice for everyone.[41] Ethiopia was just an eye-opening catalyst for me to seek out alternative retirement paths via an **economic relocation strategy**. The point is that you don't need to be rich to retire early and live in relative luxury, depending, of course, upon what you value most. You just need to be open-minded about the choices you have in life.

Alternative economic relocation strategy options

So many other countries, just like Ethiopia, have developed way beyond our perception of them. As a result, our dynamic developing world provides an increasing number of locations which offer a much cheaper cost of living than in the West, while still offering a very high quality of life. A little Internet research on my return from Africa quickly affirmed the fact that there are many people, from a range of age groups, already playing this currency and cost of living game. Some have made rather radical lifestyle changes and moved to developing countries in South or Central America, while some have made moves much closer to home.

At the time of writing in 2018, the economic situation within Europe has led to a massive fall in property prices and living costs in some of the worst effected, and ironically most idyllic places, such as Greece, the beautiful Greek islands and Spain.

For those to whom this scenario appeals, it is important to be balanced and practical if this is a serious, realistic consideration. In weighing up a move overseas, there are a number of important factors that need sensible consideration in relation to both you as an individual and the country under consideration. These include:

---

[41]   In fact, after further research I found out that, while you can live in Ethiopia, it is currently not possible for non-Ethiopian citizens to own land there.

★ Affordability — living costs and housing
★ Health care
★ Accessibility
★ Culture/ease of transition
★ Climate/weather patterns
★ Culture/things to do
★ Community
★ Connection to family and friends

This may still sound rather abstract and fanciful, so it is time to look at a specific example to see how an economic relocation strategy can genuinely work in practice, based on hard facts and a real budget.

While I appreciate that this is not for everyone, it is important to establish **the fact** that if you really want to retire right now, you really can.

Once we have established the facts, we can then move on to alternative options and strategies that are more mainstream, closer to home and likely to appeal and be realistic and practical to a much greater number of people.

CASE STUDY EXAMPLE:

The affordability of an immediate retirement
to Nicaragua, Central America

Nicaragua may not have been high on your list of countries to visit, let alone to consider relocating to, but as with Ethiopia, the modern reality is far removed from our preconceived notions. But don't take my word for it, here is what Lonely Planet has to say on the subject:

"Affable Nicaragua embraces travellers with offerings of volcanic landscapes, colonial architecture, sensational beaches and pristine forests that range from breath-taking to downright incredible."

Fortunately, the current cost of living in Nicaragua reflects the relatively recent history blighted by civil war and its location on the drug trafficking route to the US. However, since 2006, things have become much more stable and in the right areas, it now offers a very high standard of living at a very low price. For those with an eye for detail and who want to scrutinise the figures, a full breakdown is available on the Rock Star Retirement website. For those simply interested in the headline numbers that illustrate the case, here they are:

CASE STUDY A:

Burning your bridges for an **immediate retirement by liquidating your assets** (Based on a UK resident with the average realizable net worth of £147,134)

	Monthly/ Annual
Cost of living in Nicaragua (based on 2 people co-habiting), including health insurance etc. Source: internationalliving.com	$892/$10,704 £669/£8,009
Average net worth of UK adult when all assets are liquidated to cash	£147,134
8% yield on fixed return investment[42]	Generates £11,771 p. a. or £980.89/ month
Surplus	£3,762

---

[42] Please refer to the Rock Star Retirement website for up to date examples of investments offering 8% or higher guaranteed yields. Once again the author would like to reiterate that these are provided for illustrative purposes and that no investment decisions should be made without first consulting a suitably qualified financial advisor

In the example just given, the would be Rock Star Retiree has to sell their home in order to raise the lump sum required to generate sufficient passive income to facilitate an immediate retirement. In one way, this 'burning of bridges' strategy is a good thing, in that it makes it feel more final and harder to return, therefore people considering it are not going to do so lightly.

Likewise, once committed to it, people utilising this strategy are more likely to stick at creating their new life overseas and working for longer at overcoming the inevitable adjustment and teething problems. However, the flip side of this is that there is the economic risk of inflation of house prices in your country of origin while you are living overseas, making it very difficult to get back on the housing ladder if you do decide to return 'home'.

Hedging your bets for the best of both worlds

One of the really positive features about moving overseas in the early 'healthy' years of your retirement is that you can still keep some 'skin in the game' in your birth country. In other words, if you own your own home, you don't necessarily have to sell up to finance the move.

The alternative option is to rent it out to provide you with an on-going source of income in your 'strong' home currency. If you do your research, the cost of living in your early phase retirement country is going to be significantly lower than in your own home country, meaning that you may well be able to live off the income without needing to draw on any savings.

For some people, this means they can actually save money while living a fulfilling overseas retirement. With this solution, you also get the physcological advantage of a bolt hole to return to if needed. You also get the benefit of any appreciation in value to your home[43] and the ability to move back to your birth country in the later stages of retirement if

---

[43] While the long-term moving average over the last century has seen house prices increase in most areas of the UK, house prices can be cyclical and can fall as well as rise.

your health is declining, enabling you to take advantage of a more developed welfare state and healthcare system if needed.

CASE STUDY B:

Take the average UK adult's **£147,134** realizable net worth and invest it in a buy to let property.[44] This provides a passive income stream to support the cost of living overseas, while keeping some skin in the game for a return to your home country.

Value of retained UK property to provide rental income	£147,134
Typical UK rental yield on residential let	6.7% = £9,858
Letting agent fee (negotiated)	8.5% = £838
Money put aside for maintenance	10% = £ 986
Residual annual yield after costs	£8,034
Required living cost in Nicaragua	£8,009
Surplus	£25

[44] Again, this example has been simplified and is purely for illustrative purposes.

As we discovered in the introduction to this book, the house (nearly) always wins, but with this approach, you get to increase your chances of making sure that it is **your house**, not the financial services industries house which reaps the benefits.

ROCK STAR RETIREMENT TIP:

A practical consideration to ensure a roof over your head for the long-term

For people with higher than average assets invested in property, the surplus income per month will be greater, allowing for a more luxurious lifestyle. However, irrespective of asset value, ANY party considering renting property to provide a passive income stream to live off also needs to factor in periods where their property is not tenanted and therefore not producing a yield to live off. For this reason, it is advisable to build up a 'rainy day' fund of at least 6 months living costs in your relocation destination.

A crazy early retirement strategy option with a powerful psychological benefit

Irrespective of whether this is practical, or something you would ever truly consider doing, I believe that there is a significant psychological benefit of **knowing** that this is a choice that you have. These days, when I am having a really bad day, I am able to think to myself, "Stuff it, if this gets any worse I can always sell up, jack it all in and move to Nicaragua!"

For some reason, this never fails to make me smile, laugh inside and feel much better, although I doubt my wife or kids would be too impressed by the prospect! Somehow, the knowledge that you have a get out (or are working towards having enough money to have this option) is liberating, empowering and for me, also quite amusing!

An interesting concept, but what if you don't want to emigrate?

If emigration to a distant land is a bridge too far, you can still utilise the same lower cost of living relocation strategy, but on a more local, national level. Relocation within your own country from an area of high population density to a more rural area offers an alternative fast track 'Rock Star Retirement' option. House prices, rental levels and the overall cost of living are generally much cheaper in quieter backwaters, many would argue the quality of life can be far superior too.

The proceeds of the sale of a small house in London or leafy suburban south Manchester can practically buy you a country mansion in some spectacularly beautiful parts of Wales. Sell a small apartment in Manhattan and you can probably afford to buy an ex-governor's house in Mississippi. Set your sites on a more modest property in one of these beautiful, but less glamorous areas and the cash generated from the move may mean you can afford to retire in a conventional sense a decade or more earlier. Radical, but realistic.

As with the overseas relocation strategy, if you think that selling up and burning bridges is too risky, the alternative approach is to rent out your more expensive property and use the income to rent in a more rural location in your home country. This will provide you with surplus cash to spend, or save, on a monthly basis, while retaining your asset.

Should a quieter life not prove as enjoyable as you had hoped, then you can always move back to the city and you will benefit from any capital gain to the property during your longer-term ownership, although house prices (using that well-worn phrase from the financial sector) "can fall as well as rise", so this is not always a given! In the course of my work selling businesses, I have seen many, many people adopting this economic and lifestyle relocation strategy, both regionally and internationally. At the time of writing, not even one of them has returned to big city living.

But I love the area I live in, my family, friends and support network are all local — I don't want to move out to the sticks, or to the Third World

For most of us, me included, regardless of whether we actually fancy the idea or not, adopting an economic relocation strategy may be impractical. We may have dependents (ageing parents or perhaps happily settled children), or it may be that our partner does not share the same wanderlust or sense of adventure.[45] Whatever the reason, what other options have we got to allow us to retire sooner? I will answer this key question in just a minute, but first let's be really brave and put the reason why people need to find an alternative retirement strategy in some sort of meaningful context.

A conventional retirement planning example

As already outlined, the problem with financial projections is that there are so many variables. However, I hope by now that you trust me enough to let me lead you through an example of some conventional retirement planning numbers, using some mainstream assumptions.[46] If your net worth is higher or lower than the figures used in the example, it is a relatively simple process to ratio up or down the numbers provided to give you a ball park feel for your own situation.

---

[45] For older people, the thought of being far away from their grandchildren may also make this a non-starter.

[46] In the example used, the couple were non-smokers, did not suffer from high blood pressure, drank within the recommended guidelines and had a healthy BMI. For people with real life Rock Star tendencies, the good news is that bad habits get rewarded with higher annuity rate layouts, because the insurers/underwriters expect you die significantly earlier!

ROCK STAR REMINDER

You will recall that the average realizable net worth of UK adults is £147,134, but that this includes people as young as 18, who have no assets at all who distort the figures downwards. Therefore, as the following figures illustrate, the average person over the age of 50 is worth considerably more

To make this example as representative as possible, we will use a set of 'average' figures.[47]

£223,807: Average UK house price.
Source the Land Registry, October 2017

£104,496: Average pension pot for UK citizens in the 55–65 age group.
Source: Aegon in 2017

Now let's work though these figures by applying them to a fictitious couple to see what their options are:

Short-form financial profile

Name: Mr and Mrs Middle
Ages: Both 60
Retirement savings: Mr Middle **£104,496**
Retirement savings: Mrs Middle **£104,496**
Total retirement savings: £208,992

---

[47] For accuracy, I would have preferred to use a median figure, but this data was not readily available. Average is also a more widely understood term than the concept of median and standard deviation, which in the spirit of the book being jargon-free and accessible to all is easier to follow.

Property assets: £223,807 mortgage free home

Other significant assets and savings: **Nil**

They own their own home mortgage free, which also happens to be worth exactly the average.

Annuity value per annum on £208,992 at the age of 60 = £4,383 per annum[48] monthly income: £365.25
Age 65: £5,061 monthly income: £421.25
Age 70: £5,567 monthly income: £463.91

Their current UK state pension entitlement kicks in at the age of 66, but this will be increased to 67 in 2026 and to 68 in [49]2028. The income from this will be £8,094 a year, or a monthly income of £674.50.

This example has been simplified[50] but after the highs and optimism of the early retirement options of Ethiopia and Nicaragua, the numbers returned from conventional retirement planning are pretty sobering.

Don't despair, remember, that this lesson is about taking you on a journey. We have been carefully building up in readiness for this moment. Having seen the cold, hard reality of what conventional retirement planning looks like for someone of average means, I anticipate that you are likely to have experienced one of the following thoughts:

1. Shock, dismay and the wish that you had stayed in blissful ignorance within the Ostrich retirement fraternity.

2. A realisation that if you follow conventional retirement planning, you are going to have to work for an **awfully** long time and save a huge amount of money.

---

[48] Based on 50% joint life.

[49] There are no guarantees that this won't be deferred again.

[50] I have not factored in the couple continuing to top up their pension savings between 60–65 or 65–70.

3. An epiphany that Ethiopia and Nicaragua are suddenly starting to look like viable options!

4. A radical new life-plan that involves:

   a) Faking your own, or your partner's death and claiming the life insurance pay out for you both to share (with one of you living in hiding).
   b) Becoming a later-life gold digger and seeking to marry a new, very wealthy partner, or real life ageing rock star.
   c) A combination of (a) and (b)
   d) Checking out that website mentioned on page 188 and seeing what the going rate on the black market is for a kidney and what other body parts you and your partner can do without and how much money they will raise.

5. An expectation that I have something else up my sleeve.

If your response was one of the first 4 on the list, don't worry, I won't judge you.[51] If your response was the last one on the list, then you were, of course, right. So, without further ado, it is time to continue with the journey in this lesson, and to get your mood and your Rock Star Retirement planning, firmly back on track. But please note, if you fail to act having read this book, then you can't accuse me of not warning you of the potentially dire consequences to your future life.

Solving the early retirement conundrum WITHOUT a radical relocation strategy

Stripped back to basics, there are 2 preconditions that allow a radical retirement relocation strategy to work, such as the move to Nicaragua illustrated in our example:

---

[51] But I should take the opportunity to remind you that some of these activities are against the law in the United Kingdom and its protectorates and indeed pretty much throughout most of the civilised world.

1. A significant reduction in living costs

2. The generation of sufficient passive income to cover the reduced living costs

Therefore logic dictates that if a person who does **not** wish to relocate is able to achieve these same 2 preconditions via alternative means, then they too should be able to achieve a significantly earlier retirement than normal.

Let's now tackle these challenges

1. Reducing living costs without a radial relocation

Think back to lesson 8 and the exercise you completed to identify the most memorable things in your life to date. Remember too, the lessons that the Go-getters and the Humbles illustrated. Material goods do not really make us happy in the long-term, almost universally, it is shared experiences that provide us with joy and contentment.

Consider too, the fact that the clock is ticking and there may be things we want to be doing while we are still young enough, but that having to work is preventing, because we can't afford a conventional retirement. Decide where your priorities lie. All of us have areas of expenditure that could be reduced. Equally there is no point being time rich, but so monetarily poor that life is hard and lacks enjoyment because you are unable to do the things you want to be doing.

The topic of saving money is a whole book in itself and not one I personally wish to write. I have no great insights or revelations to add to the substantial body of work already out there. Making short-term sacrifices to achieve big goals may be part of the solution to get you from where you are, to where you want to be. However, living long-term on bread, water and lentils is not very Rock Star. Most of the role models from my Rock Star Retirement cohort have been disciplined with their spending during key phases in their lives, but their success and status came from being smart, open minded and adaptive in other ways.

2. Creating sufficient passive income to retire early, without a radical economic relocation strategy

Even if, unlike me, you have the discipline and inclination to live a very frugal life, there is no escaping the fact that life in Britain is much more expensive than the cost of living in Nicaragua.[52] So how can you create sufficient passive income to plug this very significant gap? Are we not moving back into the realms of 'traditional' retirement planning? The answer to the first question, is that it is certainly a challenge, but thankfully the answer to the second question is a resounding no! Let me explain:

Conventional financial retirement planning works on the basis of saving into a **dedicated retirement fund**. Therefore, mainstream projections for when you can afford to retire are based on the point at which you have saved enough into your **dedicated retirement fund** to provide sufficient passive income[53] that will cover your anticipated living cost for the rest of your life. Normally this will also factor in any state-based pension entitlement.

In contrast, the overseas early retirement relocation model, utilises one other key technique. It works on the basis of cashing in on, or utilising, **all of a person's assets** to produce a higher passive income stream at a much earlier point in a person's life. So, the conundrum is how the same

---

[52] Exact data is hard to come by, but I would estimate that is approximately double.

[53] Normally in the form of an annuity another financial services (the house always wins) product.

principal can be applied if you are not planning on a relocation, or prepared to liquidate all of your assets?

For most home owners, the value of their property greatly outweighs the value of their pension. So why not utilise this prime asset too as a core part of your overall retirement and lifestyle planning?

Time for some home truths

Of all our material possessions, our primary residence is the most significant and valuable. A house is not just a sterile piece of real estate that carries a monetary value; it is also our **home**, an ideological construct that we supercharge with emotional value.

If these four walls could talk

We feel emotionally connected to our homes because their very fabric is impregnated with the thing that we value the most, precious shared experiences. If the walls of our homes could talk, they would have some stories to tell: birthdays, Christmases, New Year's Eves, weddings, anniversaries, the arrival of our new-borns and special times with children or grandchildren. Not to mention memories of any Rock Star behaviour or transgressions that we may not want to be reminded of (there is a bit of a diva in all of us!) All of the significant events in our lives have been celebrated and experienced within our own little corner of the universe, the place we call home.

But this intangible value is not just retrospective. Our homes are also unavoidably part of the present too. Our day-to-day experience of the world is framed by our home setting. Not only within the confines of our own property and garden, but also from interactions with our neighbours and the immediate surroundings. Having great neighbours and a safe environment for children or grandchildren to play in, carries a value that is hard to quantify in terms of a transfer value; even if you move to a more beautiful home, these relationships cannot ever be exactly replicated.

An English man's home is his castle

With so much emotional energy invested, it is easy to see why, in the conventional approach to retirement planning, homes are treated completely differently from our other assets. **Yet I believe this is a massive mistake.**

We have already extensively explored the topic of radical economic relocation in terms of moving to a different country, or an alternative far flung region. But if you wish to stay where you are, then there is an alternative way to boost your retirement fund and speed up your ability to work less.

Downsizing

If you own a reasonably sized family home, then selling up and relocating to a smaller, cheaper property in the same area offers a potential Rock Star retirement double whammy:

★ The balance (after moving expenses) of the sum raised from your old larger house and your new smaller house leaves a surplus of valuable extra cash funds which can be utilised to accelerate your ability to retire.

★ Smaller properties benefit from lower running costs (reduced council tax, heating bills, maintenance etc.) resulting in lower living costs.

If downsizing appeals, but is something you think you might defer for the future, there are a number of possible variables that you need to be aware of, which could work for or against you:

★ With an ageing population in the UK, demand for bungalows and apartments is increasing much faster than the supply. This means that in many areas, these types of properties trade at a premium price already, so savings from downsizing may be less than you might anticipate. This trend is only likely to speed up, so this type of property and this downsizing option may actually not be a viable proposition. Perhaps a reason to downsize earlier? You might also benefit from a disproportionate capital appreciation on your downsized property in relation to the wider market, which you can draw down on later in life.

★ The flip side of this argument is, of course, that if you hold onto your larger family home — then you might benefit from a greater capital appreciation from which you can draw down on later.

While I am the first to admit that there is something very psychologically satisfying about living in and owning your own home, debt free and being beholden to no one, the prospect of being in the financial position to retire a decade or more earlier should I wish to, holds an even stronger draw. But what if you really, really love your home and don't want to move?

Equity release: Continue to live in your home, but use it as a cash dispenser

The value of your home, less any outstanding debt you have against it (for example secured loans or mortgages) is known as equity. So, for example:

Current value of your home:	£380,000
Outstanding mortgage:	£50,000
Secured loan:	£10,000
Your equity	**£320,000**

Traditionally this equity is usually passed on as inheritance, however this absolutely does not have to be the case. We have already looked at downsizing as one way to unlock some of the value inside your home and we have also touched on the fact that leaving the family home and neighbourhood can, for some people, be a huge emotional upheaval. Equity release schemes offer an alternative way of unlocking some of the value in your home, but without the need to move.

There are a number of different equity release products available with all kinds of features, but the 2 main types are:

1. Lump sum

Also known as a lifetime lump sum mortgage. This is a form of equity release whereby a loan is secured against your property to provide a tax-free lump sum for you to spend as you wish — normally with no monthly payments to meet.[54]

2. Drawdown

A drawdown lifetime mortgage is very similar to a lump sum lifetime mortgage, but with an added degree of flexibility. Once the maximum drawdown value of equity in your home has been agreed, it can be taken out in phases as you need it. It is, therefore, generally a more efficient way of keeping interest payments down during the early years.

If you want to consider an equity draw down on your home, this is one area that really does need review by an independent financial adviser. If you go down this route, then you are quite literally selling your own home from underneath yourself so you don't want to get this wrong and end up on the street. That said, it is a great option to have up your sleeve as a fall-back position if your Rock Star Retirement proves to be a big hit and your health and lifestyle in your old age prove to outlive the health of your finances!

To SKI or not to SKI? That is the question!

Rock Star morality, now we are talking! I could have really had some fun with the subject matter, but my editor explicitly banned me from writing a full lesson on the topic. Instead, knowing that she is such a big

---

[54] Instead compound interest is added for the life time of the mortgage until the plan comes to an end, with the loan and interest paid off on the sale of your home.

Shakespeare fan and would not be able to resist the Hamlet inspired section title (page 211), I managed to get away with this minor 7-page transgression.

For those not already aware, SKI, or SKIING in the context of later life financial planning stands for **S**pending (the) **K**ids **I**nheritance.

The key question is:

Do we have a moral responsibility to leave anything to our children/dependents? Or is it OK for us to burn through our assets to live life to the maximum in our autumn years?

For people without children and for those of more limited means, this may **not** be a consideration at all. For people possessing children and greater material wealth then just like with Hamlet's soliloquy, this can be a very difficult moral and philosophical dilemma. Like most ethical questions, the subject polarises opinion. There is no universally right or wrong answer. It is a very personal and highly emotive subject.

"There's nothing wrong with inherited wealth as long as you melt the silver yourself ...."

THE UPPER CLASSES — *The Auteurs*

The puzzle that circumstances sets and the solution to be worked out, depends upon some complex variables including:

★ your means
★ how many children/dependents you have
★ what means your children/dependents have
★ your relationship with your children/dependents

Some examples will help to illustrate the variety of scenarios and just how much of a moral maze this can be:

Scenario	Implication/likely outcome for you
Your children have already carved out their own successful careers and have amassed, or are well on course to achieving reasonable wealth independently.	This is the happiest and most clear-cut scenario. The need to worry about leaving a financial legacy for your children is less of a concern. Congratulations, its **SKI**ing time!
One of your two children has a very successful career and is already financially independent. The other has never really found their calling. They work in a minimum wage job and rent a small flat. They struggle to pay for basic living costs and you continue to have to assist them financially to help them run a car or take a holiday.	Welcome to the moral maze, a place with no definitive right or wrong answers. Do you sacrifice some of your own enjoyment of your later years by putting your children first? And if you do this, do you just make provision for the child requiring your need, or to be fair and balanced, do you also have to make equal provision for your other child, even if they don't actually need it? Whatever you decide to do is likely to be a compromise and may not feel entirely satisfactory.

You are a farmer who inherited your farm and livelihood from your parents and have in turn brought up your own children to earn their keep by working the family land.

This situation, like the first one is probably much more cut and dried.

Selling off the land to fund a lavish retirement lifestyle and leaving your children without the means to earn a living is far less morally justifiable. Instead retirement plans are much more likely to be akin to pre-pension days. The possible solution will be that your children will care for you as your ability to actively work the farm diminishes. They will support you and keep the farm generating income for the wider family, in return they will eventually inherit the asset upon which they rely to make their living.

No Skiing, but probably deeper, more intertwined relationships which carry their own very real value.

These illustrations provide an initial feel for some of the situations that can arise. There are a very wide and diverse range of possible scenarios and solutions. Some are much easier to navigate than others.

The most complex problems stem, not only from feelings of parental responsibility, but also from **parental guilt**. This parental guilt comes from a belief that we failed our children in some way by not being the best possible mother or father that we could have been. There are any number of causes of historic guilt in relation to our children:

★ We did not spend enough quality time with them
★ We were too focused on our career
★ We were too focused on keeping a perfect house and 'keeping up appearances'
★ We were too selfish
★ We spent more time with one child than another
★ We were not consistent
★ We tried to give them everything and did not push enough
★ We pushed them too much
★ We were too critical
★ We spoilt them

Whatever the cause, many people instinctively seek to wash away the guilt with money.

In my role as a business broker, I have had plenty of personal experience of helping business owners navigate the treacherous waters of intergenerational succession planning. In respect of professional confidentiality and the sensitive nature of the topic, I will not provide any specific detailed case studies. Instead, I will share a few of the questions and considerations I put to my clients to help them remain objective and to find a path through some of the complex emotional questions:

Take a step back and project what the likely impact of the different scenarios will be for both you and your potential beneficiaries.

Look at it from the perspective of your children or grandchildren. Is leaving them a significant tranche of money really in their best interests? Could it be that spending a sizeable percentage of their adult lives anticipating a windfall, or significant hand-outs along the way is actually a burden? Could your good intentions create a sense of expectation, or entitlement, that inhibits the ambition and drive of your children by preventing them from taking themselves out of their comfort zones, taking some risks and truly becoming the people they have the potential to be?

How will your feelings change towards your children, if you end up working for additional years and forgoing your own retirement dreams for the sake of them? How will you feel if you watch them make bad life choices and squander money, while you make sacrifices? How do you know they won't squander the money that you bequeath them when they eventually receive it?

ROCK STAR RISK ASSESSMENT: NEPOTISM

Nepotism is a natural instinct, but it can also have dangerous or highly destructive side effects for the 'beneficiary'. There are countless examples of real life Rock Stars and A-listers with privileged offspring, who having received material wealth and favour from their parents and as a result have taken a dark and destructive path.

Jon Bon Jovi, James Brown, Michael Douglas, Robert Downey Junior, even nice guy actor Tom Hanks, all have privileged children who have ended up with some serious problems. It is possible to kill your children or grandkids with the wrong kind of kindness.

Many people believe that rather than inheritance, a much more valuable gift you can give your children or grandchildren is quality time, mentoring and education. By providing this for them while you are still around, also means that you get to watch them benefit and blossom. With the right support in this way, they are much more likely to become financially comfortable under their own steam and more confident and independent in the long-term. We will take an in depth look at the subject of 'legacy' in the next lesson.

Depending upon your unique personal circumstances and means, SKIing may, or may not be, the right thing for you to do. The key take away message on this subject is to make sure that you think things through properly and do not fall into the trap of automatically scrimping and saving to ensure that your children, or dependents receive the maximum possible estate value at the expense of the quality of your own life. You earned it and you get to decide how to spend it.

Wow, this has been a long chapter ... we have been on quite some journey, travelling from Ethiopia to Nicaragua, then firmly back home again, we have covered Shakespeare, Skiing and some serious ethical questions, not to mention nepotism. Now it is time to pull everything together and finish off with a bang. It's time to talk about sex on the beach!

"This is not going to go the way you think"
Luke Skywalker — The Last Jedi (2017)

Sex on the Beach

Recipe

50 ml of vodka
50 ml of peach schnapps
25 ml crème de cassis
125 ml orange or pineapple juice
125 ml of cranberry juice
Crushed Ice

An orange slice, a maraschino cherry and a mint leaf for the garnish.

If you have not yet tried one, this outrageously named fruity highball is definitely something to add to your bucket list. Cocktails fit in nicely with the Rock Star lifestyle but what exactly has it got to do with Rock Star finance?

Cocktails are all about the blending … (mocktails are fine if you don't drink).

Many of the best things in life are about **fusion**, from drinks, to music, to food,[55] mixing things together to create something better than the sum of the parts.

Exactly the same principle applies to your life plan and your retirement.

ROCK STAR MUSIC GENRE FUSION HIT LIST

★ **Carlos Santana (1968)** pioneered an innovative fusion of rock and Afro-Latin rhythms to international acclaim and massive sales.

★ **Miles Davis** — transitioned from jazz to rock/pop funk with the Witches Brew album **(1970).**

★ **Red Hot Chilli Peppers (1980)**, a unique funk, metal and hip-hop blend. Their lead signer Anthony Kiedis was featured earlier in the Rock Star health section as an example of a healthy rock star.

★ **Run DMC/Aerosmith** with **Walk this way (1986)** — A timeless rap/rock hybrid classic.

★ **INXS** — **Kick (1987)** a pop-funk masterpiece album that sounds as fresh and relevant today as it did when it was released in the late 1980s.

★ **The prodigy, Fire Starter (1996)** — rock, rave, rap plus dodgy haircuts and dancing!

[55] Chicken Tikka Masala is a famous fusion of British and Indian cuisines created in the UK to provide a spicy dish but incorporating a new sauce to appeal to the British love of gravy!

★ **Mark Ronson Uptown funk (2015)** — a modern masterpiece featuring a veritable feast of sub-genres and influencers, including funk, hip hop/rap, R&B/soul, and retro. Genius!

Mixing a Rock Star Retirement Finance Cocktail to your own design

Cocktails come in all shapes and sizes, even your classic B52, Blue Lagoon, Manhattan and Mojito recipes can be tweaked to taste. Yet whether gin, vodka, tequila or whiskey-based, they are all made by mixing and blending similar basic building blocks. The same applies to your retirement options, but when it comes to creating your own unique Rock Star Retirement Finance Cocktail, we definitely don't want you to put yours permanently on ice. So, with the bad puns out of the way and the metaphor once again overegged,[56] let's look at the ingredients available to you for making up your Rock Star Retirement Recipe.

Rock Star Retirement Finance Cocktail Ingredients

Main base ingredient options

★ Traditional pension savings
★ Other non-pension savings or investments
★ Reduction of living costs[57]
★ Downsizing
★ Equity release
★ SKIing
★ State pension
★ Inheritance[58]
★ Working smarter = Reduction of working hours at an earlier age

---

[56] A real speciality of this author!

[57] Via an economic relocation strategy, or other means.

[58] If you are lucky enough to be left money by relatives who opted not to go SKIing!

Then mix in a dash of:

+ Flexible/adaptive thinking
+ Courage

The ingredients and quantities available to you will vary according to your personal circumstances and taste. The first 8 items in the core ingredients list all effectively help to create more surplus cash/income to provide an earlier 'traditional' retirement timeframe. The last item on the core list buys time in a different way, in sacrifice for income/savings.

The more ingredients you use, the earlier you are likely to be able to retire. The sequence and timing that you mix in the ingredients can be important too. The timing of, for example, the sale of a home as part of a downsizing strategy can be crucial. The housing market tends to work in cycles and selling at the peak of the market can make a huge difference.

A couple of examples will help to illustrate how this can work in real life:

ROCK STAR RETIREMENT FINANCE COCKTAIL EXAMPLES

Easy Driver/Driving Miss Daisy

Ingredients

★ Flexible/Adaptive thinking = ability to look beyond the usual, mainstream financial advice
★ Modest cash savings
★ Economic Relocation Strategy (regional)
★ Traditional pension
★ State pension (but not during the early years)
★ Continued income from reduced hours (job to die for/die in)

Future options

★ Another downsize move
★ Equity draw down on current home
★ Sale of vintage car to generate further cash[59]

Tom was a frustrated and world-weary civil servant from London whose financial adviser told him that he could not afford to retire until he was 65. Fearing he would work himself into an early grave and never get to enjoy retirement, he consulted with his homemaker wife and they decided to take matters into their own hands. A year later at the age of 57 he retired from his 'career job,' they sold the family home and relocated to a beautiful village 170 miles away. House prices there were half the price of London, so they ended up with a similar sized house with a larger garage and a much bigger overall plot size and with significant residual cash left in the bank.

Tom had always been a massive motor enthusiast, so with some spare cash and ample free time[60] he fulfilled a life-long dream by purchasing an old Rolls Royce which he renovated over a 6-month period. He then set himself up as a part-time wedding chauffer/upmarket taxi driver and later, an occasional part-time minibus/coach driver. He loves driving and all the jobs undertaken were, and are, done at his own discretion, to suit his lifestyle. The money generated allows him to change his main 'day-to-day' car every 3 years and pays for extras like holidays. Eight years later at 65 he is still enjoying taking coach loads of pensioners on day trips. He says it makes him feel young as most of his passengers are in their 80's. He and his wife are now completely settled in the local community and love the easy pace of life and the clear roads.

---

[59] Classic cars, unlike normal cars tend to appreciate over time.

[60] He would never have been able to fit a vintage Rolls Royce in the garage at his old London home.

Emancipation

Ingredients

★ A small inheritance
★ Ability to think beyond mainstream financial advice
★ Mental strength to NOT feel the need to keep up with the Joneses
★ Local economic Relocation Strategy/downsizing
★ Passive income from investment property
★ Continued income from reduced hours, at higher rates

Future Options

★ State pension
★ Company pension(s)
★ Equity draw down on current home
★ Sale/equity draw down on investment house

How the cocktail was shaken and stirred

Michael and Sharon are a couple from North Manchester. They married in their early 20s and moved into a small rented home within half a mile of Sharon's parents' house.

They had left school with few qualifications and minimal career advice and as a result they immediately drifted into low skilled, low wage work. While both had been brought up with little vocational guidance, their families had instilled in them a very strong sense of personal responsibility and pride in what they describe as "good old-fashioned honesty and hard work." Highly reliable and genuine grafters, they stood out from their fellow workers quickly becoming the "go to" people in their respective warehouse jobs. During busy periods, or if weekend or night staff were off sick or on holiday, Michael and Sharon were always the first to be offered overtime and they very rarely turned the opportunity down.

They had their first child, a beautiful baby girl in their mid-20s and within 18 months she was joined by a bouncing baby brother, completing their dream family unit.

With childcare assistance from Sharon's parents and working their shifts around childcare needs, they continued to work long hours and eventually managed to save enough money for the deposit to obtain a mortgage on a small terrace house at the age of 30.

Over the next decade, Sharon's parents aged quickly and became infirm. They not only ceased to be able to provide childcare, but also began to need help and support themselves. Then Sharon's father developed lung cancer. Sharon had to reduce her paid hours to support the needs of her parents and children.

Michael's reaction to this loss of family income was fear and his response was to pick up the slack and work even longer hours himself in order to compensate. Throughout this period, they continued to be frugal and to diligently pay their mortgage.

Sharon's father died just before Christmas 1998 and within just 4 months, her mother followed after a short illness. Sharon's parents had lived frugally in a modest rented house, so she was shocked to find that they had amassed over £55,000 of savings by the end of their lives. As their only child, she was the sole beneficiary of this money.

The couple were both physically and emotionally exhausted and Michael's long hours and Sharon's need to support her parents during their last months had meant that quality time with their own children had been almost non-existent. So the first item that they chose to spend some of the inheritance on, a family holiday, was a no-brainer. Their 2-week trip to Majorca proved to be one of the best things that they had ever done. It gave them the chance to recharge their batteries, spoil their children and make some lasting family memories. As Michael put it: *"When you go without luxuries in your day-to-day life, they feel all the sweeter for it when you do finally do get around to treating yourself. Likewise, when you work as hard as we do, you really appreciate free time when you get it."* When the children were asleep, the holiday also provided some invaluable time for the couple to sit back, take stock and reflect upon their finances and what to do with the rest of Sharon's inheritance.

Their small terraced house had almost doubled in value since they had bought it. And the fact that they had consistently used their overtime to make extra payments, meant that there was very little of their mortgage left to pay off. Clearing the outstanding debt on their home seemed a sensible move and this was the second item they agreed on. But how to invest the rest of the money? This was the hardest decision.

On the penultimate day of their holiday, Michael came across an article in the overseas version of the Daily Mail advocating that UK property has and always will be the best possible long-term investment for British families.

If they invested Sharon's parents' money in buying a bigger home, then it should be a good investment and not a risky one like the stock market. It would also be something they would enjoy every day, rather than an abstract 'financial' investment. The fact that the children would get a bedroom each, rather than having to share would have made their doting grandparents very happy and maybe they could get a larger garden too for the whole family to enjoy? The more angles they looked at it from, the more justification they found to take this path. The seed had been well and truly planted.

On their return from holiday, Michael reverted to his normal routine of shift after shift and Sharon worked as many paid hours as she could fit in while the children were at school. This meant that she had to catch up with household chores after the children had gone to bed, often working late into the night, just like her husband. Yet during this phase of their lives, neither of them minded. They both felt energised by their new mission as they began the hunt for their new family home. They were keen to put some extra money aside to pay for the moving costs to help facilitate their new dream.

Like most couples, they started their house-hunting with a sensible plan and a prudent budget. Their initial thinking was to utilise the equity from their old home, plus the cash from Sharon's inheritance to buy a larger home, but to do this "within budget" to allow them to become 100% mortgage-free. However, curiosity got the better of them and "just out of interest", they decided to take a look at a few more expensive properties to see what else they could afford if they pushed it a bit and borrowed some extra money.

Before they knew it, they had fallen in love with and moved into property in a nicer area of Manchester. A property that they could just about stretch to. It was more than twice the price of their old house and the monthly mortgage payments in the context of their typical monthly household income were scary.

For a period of time, they loved their new home. At times they had to pinch themselves that they could afford such a home, but the practicalities soon began to tarnish the experience. In their excitement, they had forgotten to account for the additional running costs of a larger home, the council tax, heat and light etc.

Now on the nicer side of town, the commute into their jobs took longer and there were often major holdups. For the first time ever, these ever reliable employees were beginning to arrive late for work. More alarmingly, they had always shared a car, with one of them walking to work. The new house was too far for either of them to practically walk to work,[61] so they had budgeted on using the local bus service. Not only did the bus encounter the same traffic bottlenecks, but it was also highly unreliable.

In desperation, the already financially stretched couple were forced to take out a loan to get a second car on the road and to leave for work 45 minutes earlier to ensure they beat the traffic. With reliability restored, both of them reverted to ever long hours of graft to pay down their scary debt levels.

Michael and Sharon were now having to graft, scrimp and save like never before and 80-hour working weeks for one or other of them became the norm.

They had a beautiful home, the children had a much larger garden to play in, but their parents never had time to play with them in it. When they were not working, then their parents were either seeking out the best possible bargains to keep living costs down or sleeping. Now in

---

[61] It was also now much further for their children to get to school, complicating the logistics of the family morning routine.

their 40s, with little time to prepare nutritious meals and with their metabolisms slowing down, they quickly began to put on weight. This pattern continued for 12 long years.

Their house might have been a dream house, but they were certainly not living a dream lifestyle. They were well and truly stuck in the rat race trap, yet against all the odds, they continued to pay off their debt. Their children left school and followed their parents lead and work ethic by quickly entering the workplace. They remained at home for a period of time and made contributions for their keep which lightened the financial burden a fraction, but for their parents, life had become one long slog.

Then everything changed. In June 2014, two events within the same month finally made Sharon and Michael wake up to the madness of their existence and lack of a life plan.

First, as part of a government initiative, Sharon's employer implemented a private workplace pension scheme for all employees. The enrolment process included a one-on-one consultation with a financial adviser. During this meeting she was briefed on how the scheme worked and to determine how much money she should pay in each month, she was asked for details of any existing retirement savings and what her pension and retirement plans were. Michael and Sharon had previously been ostriches when it came to pension planning. They had never had the luxury of spare money to even contemplate pension saving.

When Sharon discussed some initial projections with the adviser, she was stunned and disheartened by the numbers that came back. What was the point of starting to save for retirement at the age of 52? She and Michael were never going to be able to afford to retire. Based on the amount she could afford to save, the whole idea of retirement savings seemed totally futile.

Then Michael had a wakeup call of his own. He had been complaining of feeling constantly tired and breathless for some months before Sharon finally persuaded him to go for a health check at their local GP surgery. The test results that came back were damning:

★ His BMI grading was now in the obese category.
★ His cholesterol and blood pressure readings were in the danger zone.
★ To cap it all, he was suffering from a vitamin D deficiency.

Having read through the lifestyle questionnaire Michael had completed and reviewed the data from the results, the doctor pulled no punches: "If you carry on working like this and don't change your diet and lifestyle, you are going to work yourself into an early grave."[62]

Once again, just like with the previous watershed moment following the death of Sharon's parents, they decided to take some time out to have a much-needed break. This time, with no windfall to fund it, it was a more local and less exotic affair, a fortnight in Wales. Their children now had lives of their own and without the lure of guaranteed sun could not be persuaded to join their parents on holiday.

The weather was kind and they enjoyed some gentle walks, some nice meals out[63] and some long sleeps. For the first time in years, they had the space and time to take stock of their situation and options:

★ They had minimal cash savings and no private pensions.

★ They had another decade and a half before they would be eligible for the state pension — and the future amount they would receive would probably not cover the running costs of their home, let alone afford them a high quality of life.

★ This begged the question, why have a nice home, if they were going to be cold, hungry and having to work until they dropped?

★ With Michael's health now in such a bad way, if they carried on as they were, then he would have no need for a pension anyway because he was unlikely to live long enough to enjoy a retirement.

---

[62] He was also prescribed statins.
[63] Although Michael points out that the healthy options on the menu are never quite as good as the naughty stuff!

★ There was no way that either of them wanted to try and graft their way out of this problem. They were tired of grafting and besides, Michael's health could not sustain such long hours and such an unhealthy imbalanced lifestyle any more.

★ They realised that they had practically sold their lives to their jobs. Somehow, they needed to buy some time back. They had to find a way to start to work smarter, not harder.

As they started to seek solutions, rather than think about the problems, the change in their focus began to make them feel much more hopeful. The more they thought about their circumstances, they began to realise that their situation was not all doom and gloom, it was actually a much-needed wakeup call about some of their life choices and priorities:

★ They had a nice home, which like their first property had risen in value significantly.[64]

★ Their long working hours, frugal living and aggressive debt repayment meant that their mortgage was once again very small, so while they were cash and pension poor, they were actually relatively asset rich.

★ Their children were now young adults and able to provide for themselves. Like most families, there had been some challenges during their teenage years, but both children had now turned into decent young adults and both were still close to their parents. All in all, a real family success story.

★ Through thick and thin, over more than 30 years, Sharon and Michael had proven to be a strong couple and a great team.[65] While these 'family' and 'relationship' assets had no place on a normal.

---

[64] They had chosen well. Chorlton had become a very trendy 'gentrified' area with house prices rising much faster during their ownership than most other parts of Greater Manchester, especially when plans to run a direct tram service from Chorlton into the city centre were announced.

[65] They joked that they had been like ships in the night for most of their married lives and that was the secret of their marriage, because they had had minimal opportunities to argue!

financial balance sheet, or list, they considered these to be the crown jewels in terms of what they possessed.

★ Michael was not ill, he was just fatigued and unhealthy. There was no inevitability that he would get worse. A change of lifestyle could actually reverse most of his problems. Indeed, he was already looking and feeling much better only half-way through a 2-week break in Wales.

★ They had loved their family holiday to Majorca all those years before, yet they were enjoying this less glamorous and much lower cost holiday in Wales almost as much.

★ The more they looked back at and reflected on their time together, they realised that they had not been unhappy in their first home. It had been small, but they had enjoyed its cosiness. From a lifestyle perspective, the location had been great for work and the running costs and council tax were a lot lower than their current home.

★ As they played with different scenarios, they realised that if they sold up and bought a similar house to their original, this would generate significant savings that perhaps they could put towards a retirement pot to use in the future. *"Hell yes"* as Sharon commented exuberantly at the thought of the prospect: *"we could practically afford to buy two of our original homes!"*

And just like that, the solution presented itself and with a bit of further research, they hatched a bold and audacious plan to get their current and long-term life-plan back on track.

On their return from holiday, Michael cut his working hours dramatically and Sharon reduced hers too. The new rule in their household during this early transitional period was never to work more than 38 hours per week.

For the first 3 months, they used the time gained to begin some gentle exercise, to sleep 7 or 8 solid hours every night, to spend some quality time together and to cook and eat more healthy meals. The results were stunning. Within 12 short weeks as they began to retake control of their lives, they were beginning to feel like two different people. There were outward signs too as they both began to lose weight and have more visible energy and vitality. Other people began to notice, first their work colleagues and then their family, friends and neighbours. Comments like, "What is your secret?" "Have you won the lottery?", and "I'll have a bit of whatever you are on" became commonplace.

Without overtime pay and high weekly working hours their household income dropped significantly, so to plug this hole in their finances, they negotiated with their mortgage company to take a payment holiday from their normally aggressive monthly mortgage repayment. But this was just the beginning.

Four months[66] after their holiday and now feeling fully revitalised and ready to take on the world, they moved to the second phase of their plan.[67] They began house hunting close to their old home and they simultaneously began to redecorate their existing home in readiness for a sale.

Moving home is regarded as one of the most stressful events that a person can undertake in their lives, yet within 9 months of the doctor's appointment, they had successfully sold their detached home and traded it for not 1, but 2 terrace houses in the same part of town as their first home.

They chose one with a south facing garden as their new home. The second house was let out to tenants to create a passive income stream which they could enjoy now and indefinitely. Unlike buying an annuity to provide a pension income, the house would retain its value and would very likely appreciate over time. It was effectively a pension asset for today and for tomorrow, not just an abstract annual statement that they would read and worry about whether they would ever get to enjoy.

---

[66] It never ceases to amaze me how quickly people can bounce back from rock bottom to a much higher plain of existence. The common catalyst appears to be a change of mindset to take us out of "victim mode", enabling us to harness our amazing brains and the strength of positive human spirit to overcoming a challenge, rather than wallow in it. This potential is within all of us, we just have to have the strength and presence of mind to seek it out.

[67] Or "Defcon-2" as they playfully called it!

Now once again living much closer to work, they were able to sell one of their cars to reduce costs and the lower running costs of their new smaller home also reduced their monthly spending. With lower living costs and multiple income streams, they were now able to live comfortably and to put money away for a rainy day without having to work more than a normal working week.

Their plan had been executed flawlessly, but there was to be one unintended consequence that they had not foreseen. Michael's change of approach at work had not gone unnoticed. Seemingly overnight, his bosses "go to" guy was no longer interested in covering extra shifts or working overtime. Michael being Michael had, of course, continued to work diligently throughout his contracted hours, but even when the management were desperate and offered time and a half or even double time he could no longer be tempted to assist.

12 months into his new lower hours working regime, he was summoned for a meeting with the warehouse manager. His stomach was turning summersaults as he made his way to the meeting. Had their plan backfired, was he going to be put on a zero hours contract? Was he about to be made redundant? He was now 55, this was the only job he had ever had and finding another job at his age in this physically demanding world was going to be difficult. What was he going to do?

He knocked on the door, entered and was invited to take a seat by the warehouse manager. Based on Michael's account, the conversation went something like this:

Manager: "Mike, you are one of the good guys"

Michael: "Thank you sir"

Manager: "I have been looking over your personnel file and in over 35 years of working here you have only ever been off sick twice. You have been the most hardworking and dedicated employee I have ever known. However, lately, I have seen something of a change in you ......"

Michael: "Really sir, sorry sir"

Manager: "No you are misunderstanding me, I don't mean in a bad way, I mean in a good way …."

Michael: "really!?"

Manager "Absolutely. You have always done your job well, but you always used to look so fraught and on edge. If you don't mind me saying, you used to constantly look exhausted and old before your time, I was getting quite worried that I might find you collapsed on the floor at the end of the night shift! But now since you have cut back on your hours, you look about 20 years younger, but more than that, I have seen something else."

Michael "Really sir?"

Manager "Absolutely Mike, you are not only now doing your own job, but you have started to help others do their jobs better too. For the first time ever, I have seen leadership qualities in you. You have been quietly adapting the way we do things and helping other people to do their jobs better … and this is something I would very much like to harness more of. To be honest, the way you have changed is inspiring for all of us …. "

Now this was an unexpected turn of events! The top brass inspired by humble old Michael! The dialogue continued for some time as the manager wanted to know all about how Michael had changed things around.

To cut a long story short, Michael walked out of the office as the newly promoted Assistant Warehouse Manager. This involved on the job training and mentoring for him, no requirement for overtime and a significant pay rise and additional pension contributions.

Whilst he still did not mind getting his hands dirty, it was physically a much less demanding role than his old one and something that he would be able to sustain for much longer than his old role, if he wanted to. Within 6 months of his promotion, in 38–40 hours a week, he was earning significantly more than he had previously earned working 60 to 70 hours per week. Now that is definitely working smarter not harder!

These 2 case studies are just the tip of the iceberg, there are numerous ways to create your own purpose designed retirement finance cocktail. The ingredients, quantities and timing are all bespoke to you and **adaptable** to your circumstances and 'taste.'

Do you remember the Rock Star Health chapter[68] and the quote from Lao Tzu? It is well worth recapping: *"Men are born soft and supple; dead they are stiff and hard. Plants are born tender and pliant; dead they are brittle and dry. Thus whoever is stiff and inflexible is a disciple of death. Whoever is soft and yielding is a disciple of life. The hard and the stiff will be broken. The soft and supple will prevail."*

Exactly the same principle applies to your retirement and life planning. The proof of this flows through all of the case studies in this book and if you think through all of the references in your own life, you will find that it applies to your own circle of friends, family and contacts too. Stay open minded, dynamic, creative and flexible in your outlook and in your retirement thinking. Create your own unique cocktail.

For many people with lower traditional pension savings, as was the case for both families in our case studies, the solution lies in a hybrid strategy. This is likely to consist of releasing equity tied up in the family home, and a reduction in living costs, supplemented with some continued work, balanced out with lots more quality leisure time at a much younger age.

To achieve Rock Star Retirement status, the work carried out needs to be a person's own choice and done on their own terms. Therefore, ideally in your retired life, you should not really need to work to live, it should be a means of top up income to get you the money to tick off more items on your bucket list and provide a balance, some structure and some mental stimulation.

---

[68] For many readers, the Genie and the Magic Amp seem to stick in the mind as the most abstract section of this book — like some weird sort of hallucinogenic trip. Hopefully by now you will see that there was method in my madness!

You should aim to have the basics already covered. However, if you are not yet in this situation, there are plenty of alternatives. For example, you negotiate with your current employer or change to a new part-time job that lets you work Tuesday to Thursday. This way you effectively get a 4-day weekend every week, allowing you to take a long-weekend every weekend. This new employment dynamic can be extremely liberating and empowering. For people who previously worked in a professional field, there is the opportunity to do consultancy work projects with more flexibility.

In many progressive technology-based workplaces, the buzzword phrase "work life balance" is being replaced by the term "workplace integration." Cloud-based solutions, laptops, tablets, smartphones, broadband and Skype allow us to work pretty much from anywhere. As a consequence, the boundaries of where home life begins and work ends are becoming blurred. From a Rock Star Retirement perspective, if you choose to embrace this opportunity on your own terms and choose an intelligent employer then it can be a real benefit.

Having human contact with colleagues and clients can be very important, but often we do our best work when we are allowed to focus solely on one task, uninterrupted by telephone calls, emails and sociable colleagues. In many cases, working smarter from home some of the time can greatly increase productivity. I find that I can often achieve the equivalent of a full day's work in the office in a matter of hours at home. Factor in that you can save a couple of stressful hours commuting and the value really starts to show. If you produce good results, you can build up a trust relationship with your employer.

A smart employer won't mind if you go for a doctor's appointment or need to pick up your children or grandchildren during the working day, as long as you are producing great results in the quality time when you are focusing. Intelligent employers value outcomes and output rather than time on the job.

For people with valuable skills, work life integration means that you can have a sensible conversation with your employer and restructure your job to fit your desired lifestyle. You can lose the commute during peak hours, avoid certain tedious unproductive internal meetings and focus on the parts of your job that you really enjoy and are really good at.

For many people, this means that the desire to "retire' in the conventional sense may be greatly diminished for some time. If you are thinking of retiring because the rat race is grinding you down, this is a conversation you need to have with your employer right away. If your employer does not value you sufficiently, or if they are simply not progressive enough, there are niche recruitment companies which specialise in matching companies and employees up for flexible or telecommuting positions.

Do discuss your plans with a financial adviser, but make sure you set the agenda and get them to do the calculations.

For those who have genuinely fallen out of love with their career, there are plenty of opportunities to do something completely different, or to do some voluntary work to give something back. Do you remember those Jobs to Die for or Die In that I listed earlier?

I have seen countless people switch from high powered, stressful jobs to completely new and diverse work challenges that they absolutely love. These include:

★ A police inspector who, at the age of 55, relocated and **upsized** to his dream house in the country and became a gardener and an odd job man to support the running costs of his dream home.

★ A lawyer who re-qualified in his 50s to become a part-time primary school teacher working 2 days per week. To reduce his overheads, he sold his large family home for a smaller property and traded in a Porsche for a family saloon. He is enthusiastic to the point of being evangelical about telling the world that he is far happier now than when he was a flash lawyer with prestigious showpiece assets, but an unpleasant day-to-day existence.

★ A business woman who became a part-time mystery shopper.

★ A middle-aged couple who packed in their stressful jobs, sold their house and bought and ran a bed and breakfast guest house in the countryside.

Taking a balanced view

The key thing to remember is that no two lives, and no two 'retirement journeys are the same. Some people enjoy excellent mental and physical health until well into their 90s and beyond, while others can be in good health but meet a quick and premature end.

You have no idea what life has in store for you. This means that you need to design a plan for you and your finances that allows for some fun early on, but that also leaves you with enough assets to be able to enjoy a reasonable lifestyle later on in retirement if your health remains good.

The key takeaway message here is that when thinking about retirement planning, we need to think about a **whole life plan**, not just focus on the conventional retirement bit as the end game. When you do finally stop working,[69] you want to make sure that you have no regrets about sacrificing, or missing out on too much along the way.

---

[69] Some real rock stars like the idea of dropping dead on stage, going out doing what they love doing.

LESSON 9 SUMMARY

Rock Star finance

The average adult in the UK has a realizable net worth of £147,134[70]. For those really keen to retire without further delay, this knowledge provides an immediate, credible option.

A person with an average UK realizable net worth could liquidate their assets and relocate to a country with a lower cost of living to facilitate an immediate retirement. It is radical, but this strategy makes it possible to retire much younger and with a much smaller pension savings pot than via traditional routes.

For a person currently possessing lower than average realizable assets, for whom traditional pensions savings targets are so out of reach that they are prohibitive to even getting started, the lower savings target and concept of liquidating all assets to boost liquid cash, make this a much more realistic option.

We explored the hypothetical concept of a move to Ethiopia, discovering along the way that our pre-conceived ideas about what a place is like (our lens) is very often distorted, or just plain wrong. Likewise, our preconceived, preconditioned ideas about life plan and retirement options can also be unrepresentative of the truth.

For some, a radical move overseas may sound idyllic, but there are a number of practical considerations that are needed to ensure the right destination is selected and the planned move fully thought through.

For many, a move overseas may be a non-starter. Instead, relocation within your own country may provide a viable alternative accelerated

---

[70] Daily Mail article, 5 March 2014.

retirement option. Relocating from an urban area to a less populated rural area may offer similar, if slightly less dramatic, retirement living cost advantages, but with the upside of avoiding the issues of a change of language and culture, while maintaining healthcare provision.

Don't restrict yourself to traditional financial/retirement planning only. A very high percentage of many people's wealth is locked into their homes. There are a number of different ways you can access this to enjoy an earlier and more luxurious lifestyle.

Consider the children and your financial legacy to them, remember it is not a given right and it can sometimes be a hindrance rather than a blessing. Do think carefully about SKIing, or at least helping them in other ways, while you are still around.

Look at your options and create your own unique retirement financial cocktail. Remain open-minded and dynamic, be prepared to change your plans if your circumstances change.

Don't be reckless and do consult a financial adviser with your plans to ensure that they are mapped out and costed for sensibly, but don't be too conservative.

Rather than going for a big bang retirement approach, consider hedging your bets by working part-time on terms that suit you and allow for more leisure time whilst your health is still good. For many people, working for longer, but not full-time, doing something that is enjoyable, but that still creates an income, is the best of all worlds. The perfect cocktail of stimulation, structure, freedom and finance.

Fortune favours the bold and the proactive, don't be passive and leave it too long to take control and stack the odds in your favour.

LESSON 10

CREATING A ROCK STAR LEGACY

WHY BELIEF AND MEANING ARE KEY TO A SUCCESSFUL AND HAPPY RETIREMENT

When you rush around in hopeless circles
Searching everywhere for something true
You're at the age of not believing
When all the make-believe is through
When you set aside your childhood heroes
And your dreams are lost up on a shelf
You're at the age of not believing
And worst of all you doubt yourself
You're a castaway where no one hears you
On a barren isle in a lonely sea
Where did all the happy endings go?
Where can all the good times be?
You must face the age of not believing
Doubting everything you ever knew
Until at last you start believing
There's something wonderful
In you

THE AGE OF NOT BELIEVING — Angela Lansbury

THE POWER OF BELIEF

In July 2015, I was rushing to an appointment in a busy part of central London. I had arrived in the capital via train earlier that morning but had not yet had the opportunity to check into my hotel, so as well as my laptop bag on one shoulder, I was lugging a heavy suitcase with my other arm while also trying to read a map and circumnavigate the other pedestrians on the busy pavement.

It was a humid day and I was hot and bothered. I don't like being late for appointments and my inner dialogue was chastising me for letting myself fall back into the rat race, if only for one morning. It was at this most unlikely moment that I met the Yogi.

"Excuse me sir", he said, *"You have had a good life so far, but your real luck is yet to come, and it will be coming soon as you are a good hard-working man, but you think too much ..."*

The Yogi was a tall Sikh with a turban and a neatly trimmed beard, wearing an immaculate navy-blue suit. His features were striking, one of those faces that is impossible to age. He could have been 40, or he could have been 60. It was a kind face with vivid, smiling hazel brown eyes. Although softly spoken, his voice carried a wisdom and confidence that compelled me to take further notice.

It is fascinating how the human brain computes our first impressions when we interact with someone new, especially an unscheduled and unexpected interaction such as this one. The number of inputs we process, and judgement calls we make in just a few split seconds is really quite incredible.

As I listened to him a number of conflicting things ran through my mind. As with any other major world city, the streets of London contain a smorgasbord of characters. As well as the good guys, there are plenty of people looking to help part you from your money. Instinctively I glanced around me to see if he had any accomplices, but we were alone, and he stood with his hands by his sides. His body language was relaxed, open and unthreatening and he made no attempt to come closer, or to invade my personal space. The context of the meeting was not scary, we were in one of the most upmarket commercial districts in the UK.

On the one hand I was in a rush and needed to get to my appointment, but on the other, I was intrigued by this charismatic stranger. This sort of thing does not happen every day and I wanted to see where it was going. There was a strange aura about him, an inner confidence and an external warmth. My curiosity overcame my caution and my higher brain kicked in to calm my initial fight or flight instincts. Reading my face, he began to answer my unspoken questions.

"...I am a Yogi. For a lifetime, I have studied astrology and I have learned to see things that others cannot yet see. You have a very big piece of good luck coming to you soon"

As I listened to him further, my inner sceptic retuned: *"What's the scam?"*

"Am I about to be robbed?"

"Is he trying to butter me up and intrigue me to know more so that he will be able to sell me some sort of daft astrology service?"

I liked what he was saying. What was not to like? However, my caution and pressing professional need to be somewhere else ultimately prevailed and as politely as I could, I thanked him, explained that I had to be somewhere else, wished him well and extracted myself from the situation.

To my surprise, as I walked away I felt a real feeling of optimism, of hope and happiness. This feeling continued for the remainder of my 2-day stay in London. I felt on top of the world, it felt like everything was going my way. I had a new sense of optimism and the results of my meetings were spectacular. I was performing on a different level!

Even more surprisingly, when I returned home this continued. It was as if somehow on a subconscious level, I felt like it was my destiny to succeed at this time. Having had a bit of a mental block on writing my book, in the next 2 weeks I got more written than I had in the previous

6 months. The strange thing is that I am normally a very scientific, factual and rational kind of guy, but in those 2 minutes, this stranger really did influence me positively with this random interaction.

Divine intervention? Destiny? A bit of street theatre and then my life imitating the art? Or was this simply a random act of kindness, a nice person spreading the good news to help make the world a better place? Perhaps this little act had simply 'restored my faith in humanity' and my renewed drive and vigour was purely down to me feeling more optimistic.

"The harder I work, the luckier I seem to get ..."

It does not really matter where the truth lies — the fact was that I wanted to believe the words of this mysterious stranger that I was going to get my lucky break and I upped my game to ensure that it happened. I was already living a great life, I was already shaping my life with the lessons of this book, as signposted to me by my Rock Star Retirement cohort, but this was the extra push I needed to get the book closer to the finish line.

That strange encounter with the Yogi also gave me another focus. Since that meeting, I have been working on replicating what happened to me that day. How to give other people a similar, positive 'nudge', to help them feel that they too are on the verge of getting their break and hitting their goals. Giving them a sense of positive expectancy that if they make the effort to take stock, make a plan and put some work into implementing the plan then the positive change, the *good luck* will come for them too.

So, if you are not fortunate enough to have a brief meeting and a narrow escape from a random Yogi, how can you get yourself in the right mindset?

Well, I do happen to know the answer to this, because life is not some breezy thing that just happens. The positive effects of the Yogi lasted a few weeks, but then life's ebb and flow took hold again. Real rock stars and aspiring rock star retirees do have good days and bad days, days where we are proud of ourselves and days when we well and truly fall off the wagon.

Every so often, I have to give myself a serious pep talk.

I would love to claim credit for the technique that works for me, but once again, it is something that I copied from a far wiser man than me. He taught me that, rather than wait for the rock star retirement train to really come off the rails, instead to build in a regular maintenance plan into your life. This way as the wheels on the rolling stock start to creek, they get a little oil before they rust up and completely seize up.

My mentor taught me to take at least half a day out, every 3 months, with a quality block of time dedicated to reviewing how things are going with my own life plan. A critical part of this 'audit' day is to take yourself completely out of your normal environment. This not only avoids distraction, but also provides stimulation and context against which to reflect.

When I first did this, it was way outside my comfort zone and it felt both odd and self-indulgent. I was busy and simply did not have the time, but my mentor was insistent that I make the time. His assertion was well founded.

Building this process into my life has helped me to consistently achieve so much more than ever before and to keep me happy and focused on the right things, meaning that the investment of the time is more than justified.

I now thoroughly look forward to these "audit" days, they keep me accountable and my flight plan on track, allowing me to make any adjustments as needed. I have tried a variety of venues, such as coffee shops, libraries and even country parks during the summer months when the weather has allowed it.

Best of all, I have found museums and art galleries to be the perfect environment. Architecturally they are inspiring spaces, but beyond this, these venues house thousands of priceless artefacts, showcasing the scale, depth, ingenuity and history of ways that man has created to express himself. Works of art, created or commissioned by people often long dead, made to leave a lasting testament, a permanent mark or a legacy for the person who made them or funded their creation. When you take a little time to reflect in a gallery environment packed with these artefacts, it gives a true sense of perspective on the fact that we are just passing through. You and I are just one of the billions of humans that have and will inhabit planet earth.

Take a look at people, rushing around, taking selfies and photos, updating social media, trying to be seen to be seeing as much as possible, but often actually taking very little in!

Environments like museums and art galleries highlight both the brilliance and futility of man. They are a great place to think about yourself and where you fit in the greater scheme of things and to update progress on your life plan. You are both significant and insignificant, unique, yet one of billions. When your time is up, what will your legacy be and how will people remember you?

Remember, it is important to have a purpose and goals WHATEVER your age, but it is also important not to take yourself TOO seriously. Purpose and fun are not mutually exclusive. I believe that purpose without fun equals pompous! I think that a brilliant comedian's art is equal to that of any critically acclaimed master painter or poet.[71] Someone who has lived a happy fulfilling life with few regrets is as valuable as someone who has achieved a position of high status but has trodden all over people to get there.

Risk versus Reward

I must at this point stress that having a positive, optimistic and giving outlook is not rewarded or reciprocated 100% of the time unfortunately. My Rock Star Retiree cohort warned me of this and their advice has proven to be accurate in my own experience and at my own expense. Sometimes our trust is abused and our faith in others is ill-founded. Not

---

[71] The Old Masters' works may be worth millions but looking at their work does not give their audience those amazing feel-good endorphins that laughter produced by listening to a comedian, or to great rock music, can.

everyone out there is a good egg, however, maintaining a positive outlook on life strongly outweighs being a pessimist and a cynic.[72]

Personally, I would much rather live a life less ordinary, a life with passion and giving with soaring highs and the odd low. More often than not, when I have shown faith in others, or done a good deed for someone, I have been paid back in spades. There is one particular story I would like to share that illustrates this.

A near miss with royalty

A short while ago, I was asked to assess the value of a business in London with a view to an imminent sale. After a couple of hours on-site with the very emotional owner, it was very clear she was having a really hard time. She had only owned the business for a few years, but her circumstances — including having a baby and having to move overseas with her high-flying husband who worked for the British government — had significantly reduced the amount of time she was able to invest in the business. When you factored in what she had originally paid to buy the business, what she had spent on cosmetic and infrastructure improvements, and what the business was now worth, she was in for a significant loss.

Even worse, having sacrificed the performance of her enterprise to support her husband, she had not been able to do herself justice and felt like a failure. Rather than charge her for a written valuation report, I provided her with an informal assessment of the situation and an overview of options and scenarios.

It was clear that she had unfinished business and that with the right support — and now that she was back in London and able to dedicate more time to the business — she could turn things around, dig herself out of a hole and turn failure into success. I provided her with a few

---

[72] With the exception of taking "The News" as reported by the mainstream media in good faith. As I have been at pains to advocate, please do use sufficient objectivity and cynicism when it comes to how news is reported.

initial pointers and stayed in touch over the coming months, providing free mentoring and some additional business resource to try to keep her on track.

About 6 months later my firm was exhibiting at a 3-day trade show in London. One afternoon she unexpectedly came onto our stand and invited me to join her and her husband for dinner that evening. Slightly unusually, she arranged to pick me up from Notting Hill tube station.[73]

After the show I rushed back to my hotel, showered, changed and via my laptop remotely logged into my office computer system to bring up the file and remind myself of the financials of the business and the advice I had provided to date. I was sure that my "client" wanted to talk through things with her husband. Perhaps now that things were improving, they wanted an updated valuation with a view to selling the business?

Although in a rush, but not wanting to turn up empty-handed, I quickly found an off-licence on the way to the tube station, grabbed and paid for the nearest bottle of red wine and caught the tube. As my train hurtled westwards deep under the streets of London, I briefly reflected on why the cashier at the off-licence had given me such a wry smile, but this was quickly forgotten, as I used the time to focus on continuing to review the different scenarios for my client.

To my surprise, I actually arrived early at Notting Hill Gate station, relieved, I took the escalator and headed for the nearest exit ready to be picked up. The only problem was that, like many London tube stations, there was a warren of different exit options leading to different streets and different sides of the road throughout the vicinity. As I was still a fraction early, I put the postcode of my host into the Google maps app on my phone and discovered that it was only a 5 or 6-minute walk away. With the London traffic and the difficulty of turning a car around on busy streets it seemed more sensible for me to walk, so I texted my client and asked for the rest of the address. She phoned me back almost straight

---

[73] In London the traffic is so bad that people rich and poor tend to use the subway system to get around, but at the time we made the arrangements, I had had a long day and did not really have time to think about it.

away and told me that, due to security at the end of her road, I would not be able to gain access past the police and that she would therefore need to pick me up. At this point my mind began to wonder whether there had been some sort of terrorist attack, or other security incident, in central London.

After another call to better establish my whereabouts, my client finally picked me up. Her car was comfortable, but nothing special, a high specification mainstream vehicle with 2 children's seats in the back. Years of working with people, both rich and poor, have taught me that cars are a pretty poor indication of wealth in any context.[74] My main memory of the car was that the back was a mess with all of the paraphernalia of having young children and that from my own experience, the leather seats were a good investment to cope with the inevitable spillages and accidents of family life.

The car journey to the end of her street took less than 3 minutes and it was some street, a very wide, private avenue, more of a boulevard really, separated from the public roads by high metal fencing. The entrance was guarded by a full-on military gatehouse with the double protection of a gate. Steel bollards beyond that retracted under the ground to permit authorised traffic. A stern-looking military policeman, a submachine gun over one shoulder, came to the window and shone his torch first at my client and then proceeded to scrutinise a security pass she presented. My mind began to wonder, what was her husband's job? Was one of them a spy? A diplomat or an ambassador?

Recognising my client and being satisfied with her identification card, the policeman then turned his attention and his torch to me. I swallowed hard and felt instantly nervous. Why is it that, despite being law-abiding and having nothing at all to worry about, I always feel tense, almost guilty in these kinds of situations? What felt like a good minute was probably no more than a few seconds, but finally he moved his torch to sweep the back of the car and, satisfied that we presented no threat, he wished us a pleasant evening and signalled to his colleague in the

---

[74]   I have seen plenty of people with flashy cars and massive debts and plenty of people with modest cars and massive bank balances!

gatehouse. The gate rose, the bollards retracted, and my host wound up the window smiling to herself, quietly enjoying my bewilderment.

As we began to drive down the road, my host began to point out some of the mansions as we passed them. They seemed to get bigger the further down the road we travelled. It was all a bit of daze, but I remember the Lebanese Embassy, the official residence of the high commissioner of India, Russian oligarch and Chelsea Football Cub owner Roman Abramovich's home, Indian steel magnate and the135[th] richest man in the world, Lakshmi Mittal's mansion and also Kensington Palace Gardens being pointed out, which in my excited state of mind, I vaguely recalled as having some connection with the late Princess Diana.

Having enjoyed leaving me bewildered for long enough, my host decided the time was right for the start of an explanation of sorts, modestly declaring: *"We are very lucky Dominic, we are living somewhat above our station ... our apartment comes with my husband's job as part of his reward package..."*

Half a mile on, with questions still dominating my thinking, the mansions ended, and we reached the end of what I now know is referred to as Billionaires Row. We slowed down and turned into a much narrower tree-lined drive. Our way was once again obstructed by a sizeable guard house and again we had to go through a pretty stringent security check before we were finally cleared and off on our way again. By this point my mind was racing with questions.

Who or what on earth could be more exclusive and require even more security than all those embassies and residences accommodating some of the world's richest and most influential individuals? My brain began to come up with even more outrageous hypotheses about where I was going and who my client really was:

Was I about to be recruited by MI5?

Had I caused some sort of diplomatic incident back in Ethiopia that needed to be rectified after I had gate-crashed the stage at the Hilton Hotel in Addis Ababa to get a photo with my hero, the legendary Haile Gebrselassie?

Sorry for the bad image quality. Image taken from CCTV/ security footage of the author photo bombing legendary Haile Gebrselassie on stage pre-race in Addis Ababa, Ethiopia

I got the distinct impression that my host was somehow enjoying my bewilderment. A minute or so later, we finally pulled to a stop next to a number of very expensive looking Range Rovers at the rear of a large complex of buildings. Architecturally these buildings were very different, a much older style than the other buildings we had passed. My host took the keys out of the ignition, turned to me and with a sparkle in her eye nonchalantly said: *"Welcome to Kensington Palace!"*

Now my friends will vouch that I am in no way a wine snob, but — and I know it is ridiculous — the first thing I thought at this point, pushing all of my conspiracy theories to one side was: *"I wish I had spent a bit more time and money picking out a better bottle of wine to have with dinner at Kensington Palace!"*

Before this moment, I had not really had a chance to examine what I had bought. I had been far too busy preparing for a business meeting and then gawping wide-eyed at the amazing street, so as we got out of the car, I glanced down at the bottle of wine in my hand. Oh, dear God! My heart skipped a beat as I took in the picture on the label. This was going to go one of two ways. The wine was either going to be received well and seen as a bit of fun. Or, on the other hand, depending upon who the other guests were for dinner, I was quite possibly about to create another diplomatic incident. The label featured a brash illustration of an aristocratically dressed amphibian sporting a beret, blazer and breaches and to my abject horror, the wine was called "Arrogant Frog!"

As we walked from the car, I did seriously consider quietly discarding the bottle behind a plant, but before I had the opportunity, we had reached our destination. My host unlocked a surprisingly normal looking front door and we went straight into a largish kitchen. There was no butler to greet us and no chefs preparing some elaborate 12-course banquet. Instead, I was introduced to my host's partner, who was putting the final touches to our meal, a hearty looking chicken dish.

There was no conspiracy or elaborate plot and unfortunately my country did not need me. Instead I spent a lovely evening in great company and without international incident; I was the only guest and my hosts were clearly not Francophiles. Despite the preparation I had done, my invitation was not even anything to do with business, it was simply a thank you meal for my efforts in the previous months to help them with their business planning.

And the reason for the prestigious address? My client's husband had been a very high ranking and decorated officer in the British Army who now worked at the very top level at the Ministry of Defence. His role was liaising between the Government[75] and the British Army. He was a very down to earth and affable host and I gleaned most of the impressive details of his CV via his wife and by online research afterwards (when I checked him out afterwards he even has a Wikipedia page dedicated to him outlining his distinguished military career.) His wife also let it slip that they had entertained the then Prime Minister, David Cameron, at the same dining table where we ate, only 3 months prior to me.[76]

What I did find out more freely on the night was much more about Kensington Palace and its residents, past and present. My earlier association of Kensington Palace Gardens with the late Princess Diana had been right, Kensington Palace (or KP as she used to refer to it) had indeed been her residence from her early years of marriage to Prince Charles and she had remained there after her divorce until her tragically premature demise. However, her legacy at KP remained. My host's

---

[75] Ministry of Defence (MOD).

[76] Apparently her children played up that night and kept interrupting the highbrow dinner conversation much to the PM's disdain!

current next-door neighbours were none other than Prince William, Kate and baby George!

While I did not actually have dinner with royalty, I did have dinner with the next-door neighbours of 2 future kings, the 3rd and 4th in line to the British throne, which I think is still pretty cool. And I did get to hear some hilarious stories about the royal toddler's interactions with my host's children in the private grounds.

The other stand-out memory of this unexpected dinner was when I was admiring an epic looking oil painting of a historic tall ship in majestic full sail, only to be told that the canvas has actually been painted by one of Captain Cook's crew who was present during the discovery of Australia. The painting was pretty good, but the context and history behind it just made it amazing. What a legacy!

Beyond revealing my over excitable imagination,[77] there are a number of things that this story and my experience illustrates:

You reap what you sow — by helping someone in need and providing time and service without expectation of payment, or return, often carries its own reward, especially when genuinely least expected. In this instance, I was rewarded by something far more valuable and memorable to me than financial gain. I was given privileged access to a very private road and allowed to enter a world normally reserved for diplomats, billionaires and royalty for a truly money can't buy experience.[78]

Be the reason to make someone smile today and the world will smile back

When I described my host's apartment at Kensington Palace as being next-door to the heirs to the throne, I meant it. Without any concept of status or position, the toddler prince and my host's children naturally gravitated towards each other, and in the same way that countless

---

[77] And far too similarities for my own liking between me and Rowan Atkinson's portrayal of calamitous Johnny English's penchant to risk and create international incidents.

[78] Unless you are a billionaire and can afford to buy a house on the private road.

parents have become acquainted with other parents while their children played together, they slowly built a friendship.

It is widely reported that Princess Diana in her early years of marriage felt lonely and isolated living in the bubble that is being a royal in the exclusivity of Kensington Palace. I strongly suspect that an insightful civil servant recognised the same risk to the next generation of royal spouses and carefully selected a suitable grounded couple with good character and young children as neighbours to help bring some normality within the Royal Bubble.

Whilst I did not get to meet the royals, it was fun for me to expand my own normal frame of reference and to get such a privileged insight into this world!

"Twenty years from now you will be more disappointed by the things that you didn't do than by the ones you did do.
So, throw off the bowlines.
Sail away from the safe harbor.
Catch the trade winds in your sails.
Explore. Dream. Discover"
MARK TWAIN

Legacy

A great way to determine how happy and fulfilled a person feels, is to ask them to think about their *legacy*. In its most common usage, legacy is a legal term referring to money and other assets that will be gifted to a person's heirs.[79] Type the word legacy into a search engine and it is this context that will dominate the results. This is because, as we have already seen with other financial services, there is significant money to be made from legacy planning. We have already dealt with the moral conundrum of whether to leave a financial legacy in the — To SKI[80] or Not to SKI section, so instead, we will focus on the other aspect of legacy.

As important, but more difficult to define or quantify, is a person's **non-material legacy**. It is the mark that they leave on the world, what difference they have made, their relationships and how they have influenced and made other people feel.

"Legacy is not just about leaving something for people, it's about leaving something in people"

---

[79] As you know by now, this is not something an aspiring Rock Star Retiree should have as their primary focus.

[80] SKI = Spend [the] Kids Inheritance.

Exercise:

Q: If you got run over by a bus tomorrow and departed this mortal coil, what would your legacy be at this point in time?

(There are no right or wrong answers here, so don't be shy.)

_____

_____

_____

_____

_____

Personal legacy is **not** a metric that your financial adviser will have discussed with you. People often feel a touch melancholy as they begin to consider their life from this more philosophical context.[81] The exercise you have just completed may have highlighted unfulfilled objectives and perhaps regrets about how parts of your life have been lived, or how you conducted yourself in certain relationships. Yet this is no bad thing, because this exercise records perception of your <u>current</u> legacy. It is a measure of how your life has been lived so far.

For those of us lucky enough to be alive and able to carry out this exercise without the need of a spirit-medium or Rock Star genie, this means that we all have the ability to create a future legacy. We simply need to avoid that bus so that we can write our own legacy going forward.

---

[81] This would definitely be the case for Frank and the Go-getters!

Be someone who leaves a mark, not a scar

As already highlighted, not all aspects of a person's non-material legacy are good. A bullying management or communication style in the workplace can destroy the confidence and quality of life of colleagues.

If your parents were worriers or pessimists, it is very likely that they passed on some of this trait to you and the chances are that, unless you are very careful, you too will pass on this learnt behaviour trait to your children as part of your legacy to them. However, simply starting to think about your legacy can have a profoundly positive effect on these types of behaviours. Recognition and admission of guilt are a big part of the cure. But enough about the bad stuff, what about our more positive non-material legacies?

Many of the games you play with your children or grandchildren are most likely learnt; your general style of play and your sense of humour, almost certainly replicate one, or a combination of both of your parents and form part of their legacy, and yours. Indeed, children are often a person's most obvious legacy, the biggest impact that they have on the world and the legacy that will persist the longest, generation after generation.

Most people who undertake the legacy exercise for the first time naturally focus on the significant, most obvious elements. In doing so, it is easy to overlook many of the smaller things which are equally valid. Some examples might make this a little clearer and help you to see that your legacy is probably *already* much greater than you realised.

Are you still using granny's amazing apple pie recipe? Although she may be long gone, her legacy is very much alive and well, making your house smell fantastic when you use it and creating some special family moments, as well as your own food culture legacy when you too share it with your own family.

Unlike real life rock stars, we can't all have a platinum selling record to our name, but there is a whole raft of our own sports, music, arts and academic achievements that do form part of our legacies.

These don't have to be world class achievements. As already mentioned, my sister's name will forever be engraved on the lower flute cup at Matlock convent, admittedly there were no other children playing the flute in her school, but she is very proud of the fact that this forms part of the Watson family legacy and within our family culture, this remains the highest musical achievement to date over 4 generations of Watsons.

These achievements don't all have to relate to your youth either, I won the ICBA student of the year award at the age of 39, but this was nothing compared to my Mum who started Spanish lessons and achieved a Spanish GCSE in her 60s (she has now read the book and reminded me of this!).

Modern technology means that there are more opportunities than ever to create innovative new forms of legacy. At the age of 45, I am currently using a GPS Garmin running watch and an online athletics app called Strava to leave times with my name against them on virtual running routes[82] located all around my village and the surrounding countryside. I hope my sons will enjoy trying to beat their dad's time on these routes in their late teens and early 20s!

It's a musical journey and it's all in the mind

Most successful long-lived rock acts go on some form of spiritual journey during the lifetime of their musical career. The Beatles famously hooked up with Yogi Maharishi Mahesh and returned from India playing the sitar and adopting yoga and transcendental meditation!

As we saw earlier, the singer of The Police and platinum selling solo artist Sting transitioned from being a rock star junkie to a health freak. This corresponded with him finding a conscience and becoming a champion for the preservation of the rain forests and a notable environmentalist. More recently Cold Play frontman Chris Martin appears to have adopted elements of the hippy movement into his song writing and lifestyle. Indeed, these days it would seem that every rock, pop and

---

[82]   Called Strava segments.

movie star seems to have to publically hire a shrink as some sort of rite of passage. But this is NOT for you. Successful rock star retirees seek out inspiration and sort out their own heads.

A Reminder: Choose Your Template Carefully

As I have already alluded to, in my career, I have worked with some extremely 'successful' people in a traditional sense, but who I hold no desire whatsoever to emulate. These are people whose success is measured in a purely commercial, net worth, monetary sense; people who are rich in possessions and status, but poor in happiness, poor in time and often poor in personality (if not sometimes downright awful).

So, what should our legacy look like?

As with the whole Rock Star Retirement concept, there is no single, one size fits all answer. It comes down to your personal preferences, culture and wider belief systems. Your ultimate legacy should be whatever will give you comfort and satisfaction that you are making a difference. It may be a big significant difference, impacting on large numbers of people, or a small one impacting on a single individual. Both are worthy, as long as they are genuinely yours and provide you with satisfaction.

A Rock Star Publishers Story and Legacy

English publisher and philanthropist Felix Dennis (1947–2014) was a larger than life character and very much a one-off. I include him as an example of the importance of legacy, not as a blueprint for how to live your life. His full life story has been well documented and is worth adding to your reading bucket list, but here is a quick summary. Very aptly he started out with rock star aspirations, playing in a number of R&B bands, but his success and fame were destined to come from an entirely different field, publishing.

His entry into the sector started with magazine distribution, which he quickly supplemented by writing his own material. Early achievements included the first ever review of Led Zeppelin's debut album and a detailed biography of Bruce Lee, including very personal interviews with the great man's family published just prior to Lee's death. Felix Dennis quickly applied everything he had learnt to produce his own edgy magazines, frequently getting in trouble with the law with accusations of *conspiracy to corrupt public morals*. However, it was his edginess and sense of timing of what was on trend in popular culture that made his publications stand out from the crowd.

Through further organic creativity of new magazines and reinvestment of profits into the acquisition of established publications, he rapidly created a substantial portfolio of cash-generating titles. Prior to his death, he remained sole owner of Dennis Publishing, which possessed around 50 publications and websites including Auto Express, PC Pro and Viz.

I will leave it for you to decide whether Dennis was a nice man or not, but his legacy includes being credited as the first person to drop the C-bomb on live television[83] and describing himself as "an amoral sod."

His best-selling book, "How To Get Rich[84]" also revealed another dark legacy, the confession (or perhaps boast) of having spent over $100 m on crack cocaine and women! His had an undeniably hedonistic rock star lifestyle, with the danger of the self-destruct button being pressed throughout his life. However, during the latter years of his life, there was a clear reflection on his legacy and a pressing desire for his success and his life to be more, to mean more.

Following the success of his 2006 book, works of poetry followed and he took these on the road and became a successful live performer, albeit arriving at his live reading gigs in a helicopter just like the rock star that he was!

---

[83] Dennis was credited with having been the first person to say the "c" word on live British television. On 7 November 1970, during an edition of David Frost's The Frost Programme.

[84] Dennis, Felix (2006). How to Get Rich, Ebury Press.

In 1995 Dennis planted his first forest, an act that seems to have provided him with a deep and lasting sense of fulfilment. Having discovered that the UK is one of the least forested countries in Europe (13% covered by forest, compared with an average of 37% across Europe) and with a high percentage of British woods being made up of non-native species, the desire to improve this situation quickly turned into a burning passion.

Dennis had finally found real purpose and a way of building a significant legacy. By the time of his death the milestone of having 1 million native trees planted had been achieved, with £5m of his financial legacy also bequeathed to maintain and expand the forest for the enjoyment of all, for centuries to come. As a result, Felix Dennis will now go down in history as a hedonist with a heart, rather than solely for his association on various levels with the C-bomb word!

Take Stock Now To Avoid Retrospective Realisation

I worked with an elderly and very wealthy client over a decade ago, and he once invited me to his home. Purpose-built in the mid 1960's, it could have doubled perfectly as a Bond villain's lair, a vast modernist structure of concrete, glass and steel, built deep into a hillside. Flat-roofed and full of straight lines, function over form.

Externally, it was certainly no architectural classic, it was the sheer scale that impressed. The kitchen, walk-in larders, laundry room, games room, gym, formal lounge, dining room, cinema room, library, study and snug were all on the upper level. The 6 bedrooms, each with a substantial en-suite bathroom, were all on the lower level, as was the piece de resistance, a combined pool, sauna and spa room boasting retractable glass walls opening onto a terrace with panoramic views of the 2-acre garden below.

My client spent so long showing me around his mansion, highlighting the details of its design and construction that he appeared to have forgotten the real reason for our meeting. It is now something of a blur, but I do recall mention of Italian granite work tops, teak balustrades and state-of-the-art, triple glazed glass from Germany.

He clearly took immense pleasure in his house and the grand tour took so long that I had to remind him to take me to see his business which I had come to value. However, the most memorable thing about our meeting was when I enquired about whether he had any other family. He revealed that he had 2 grown-up sons. The eldest he described as doing 'pretty' well, while the youngest was doing 'astonishingly' well.

Based on just how impressive his house was, I could not help but wonder what doing *astonishingly* well might look like in terms of lifestyle! As we talked about his motivation for the sale of his business and what he planned to do with the money, we got onto the subject of trusts and inheritance planning, all pretty dry stuff. However, as he talked through the details of the trusts, he revealed that between his 2 sons, there were also 4 grandchildren and it was the grandchildren who were the planned beneficiaries of most of his wealth.

As he talked about his wider family, he became more animated and his eyes shone noticeably brighter as he asked me if I would like to see some photographs. He reached into a large wallet and pulled out a couple of small portrait photos and passed them over to me with excited anticipation. Fully expecting to see studio shots of cute grandkids, the subjects on the photos came as something of a surprise. The first appeared to be, to my untrained eye, a medium sized super yacht moored somewhere in the Mediterranean. The second was an external shot of a private jet plane. As my jaw dropped, he explained that these were his youngest son's 'babies!'

Yet when I commented about how lucky his actual grandchildren were, his shoulders visibly sagged, and a look of real sadness took hold of his face. For the next few minutes I felt like a priest hearing a confession as he decided to tell me all about what was troubling him.[85] It transpired that he had not seen his grandchildren for over a year, due to a falling out with his sons. As he reflected on how this situation had come about, he became increasingly melancholy.

He admitted to having spent most of his life pursuing what he described as "the dream." Chasing "shiny things, objects of desire and the accomplishment of status and recognition." He had worked obsessively, with his business and career and the fruits it bore, leaving very little time for anything else in his life. He had sent his children to boarding school from the ages of 8–18 to provide them with a great education, (and I suspect to stop them getting in the way of his work or messing up his show house.) As a result, he had spent very little time with them. Even during school holidays, he had worked obsessively at building his business.

Benefitting from a privileged education from one of England's top boarding schools and using Dad's example, his sons had followed his lead, each competing obsessively to be the most successful in their own fields. History repeated itself and they too sent their children to boarding school. However, with the wisdom of age and in the early stages of the 'final analysis', their father had started to realise that there were more important things in life, a fact that he had tried to convey to his own boys, to help them benefit from his new perspective.

This did not go well, there were clearly some repressed abandonment issues and they were furious that he had the audacity to try to tell them how to raise their children, having emotionally neglected them during their own childhoods. They had been starved of parental attention and love and felt that he was being very hypocritical. They also had no point of reference and did not know how to be demonstrative in this way with their own children. He was now in poor health (the reasons for the planned business sale) and in the early stages of his own final analysis,

---

[85] This seems to happen to me an awful lot in my professional career. Although trained as a business consultant, I often feel more like a counsellor. Another sure sign that status and the trappings of success often don't lead to happiness. Another compelling driver for me to write this book to get the message out there to give these guys a useful legacy.

the picture was not pretty. "Dominic, if I could go back now and change things, I would. All of these things", he said, pointing at his mansion "mean nothing. I would give them all up in an instant to have a closer relationship with my children and grandchildren ..."

PARANORMAL LEGACY?

While you may not be able to match Felix Dennis's epic forest legacy, or a real rock star's culturally significant legacy, at least your own legacy is unlikely to be tampered with after your demise! In December 2006, the BBC produced a programme called *Duet Impossible*. It featured a number of posthumous duets between deceased legends and current stars. The unlikely combinations included:

Dusty Springfield (1939–99)
singing *Dancing In the Street* with the Sugarbabes

Roy Orbison (1936–88) singing Pretty Woman with Westlife

Eva Cassidy (1963–96) singing
Somewhere Over The Rainbow with Katie Malua

Desecration of a musical legacy or the ultimate compliment? Without the aid of a Rock Star Genie, I guess we will never know what these legends would have thought!

Why legacy is important

The concepts of legacy and purpose are intertwined. We look at them to seek meaning in our lives in an effort to make some sense of it. Building a legacy means giving ourselves a sense of purpose. As Felix Dennis illustrated, even if you really can have it all, a 100% hedonistic lifestyle is still not enough!

The Cost of Grand Designs—A Lesson from a Rock Star Architect

While shooting high and aiming for a significant, long-lasting legacy is admirable, it does come with a health warning. Big success in terms of legacy-building comes at a price. This is a fact that working with my most successful clients showed me, but something that despite the warning, I have still chosen at times in my life to endure for the greater good.

Many of my clients are self-made men and women who have built multi-million pound businesses from scratch. Businesses built with passion and integrity, offering great products and great service. Businesses that are run by happy, motivated staff, brilliantly serving customers.

However, achieving this type of business success does not happen overnight. More notable achievements generally take significant hard work, a combination of effort, focus and time. As we have already seen, time and in particular *quality* time, while in good health, are precious.

BIG projects devour BIG personal resources

Most people are familiar with the TV programme Grand Designs. If you have not seen it, it is broadcast by Channel 4 and focuses on couples who set out to build their own dream home. Frequently multi-year projects, the programme documents the trials and tribulations of these mammoth undertakings which the rock star architect and likeable presenter, Kevin McCloud keeps tabs on as the project unfolds (and very often unravels.)

Almost all of the projects end up taking longer than anticipated and most are significantly over budget. To fund the creation of their dream home, the couples often have to sell their existing accommodation and move into a caravan on site or live with relatives.

As well as holding down full-time jobs, or fulfilling normal parental responsibilities, the couples usually have to both project manage and put in significant labour and hard graft themselves. Financial concerns, being let down by contractors, cramped and compromised temporary living conditions, stress and minimal free time, all contribute to points in the project where the situation looks close to breaking point. Invariably the couple usually pull through and succeed in the project, coming away with a beautiful house, a deeper relationship and a sense of immense fulfilment, but almost unanimously they admit that the price they had to pay was far more than they had ever envisaged and that they had made a number of short-term compromises on the quality of their lives while building their dream home.

This reality is not limited to house-building, it holds true for any other Grand Designs you may have for your legacy, like writing a book for example!

As I write this section and the end is in sight, it has taken me more than triple the time I had expected to reach this point. While at times, I have really enjoyed writing, at others it has proven seriously challenging as I have had to sacrifice sleep and the enjoyment of other aspects of my life, including less quality time with my wife and family, to keep the project on track. Sometimes in life you have to make this kind of short-medium term sacrifice, a reasoned delayed gratification strategy, just make sure that you don't fall into the ultimate delayed gratification scheme called the traditional pension planning system. As already pointed out at some length, this route is just too risky to take.

2 Lessons in 1

So, you think you have been dealt a bad hand? Feel the odds are stacked against you? Experienced bad luck? The truth is that whether you are a Rock God inhabiting the spotlight on centre stage, or currently reside firmly in the cheap seats; life does not distinguish or discriminate. All of us, and I mean **all of us**, suffer setbacks. We all get the odd bottle thrown at us and experience our lives going off-key at some point. Despite external appearances, life is rarely smooth for anyone **and I mean anyone!**

"A person who never makes a mistake,
is a person who will never
make anything worthwhile"
ALBERT EINSTEIN

At some point in our lives we make mistakes or get let down by someone we love or trust, we will suffer from ill-health and will all lose at least one loved one. This is not meant to be depressing, it's just the harsh truth of life. What distinguishes us is how we deal with what is thrown at us.

How I Met Cody

Despite some of the amazing things I have been privileged to experience, I am naturally quite introverted. When I first meet new people, I can be quite awkward and shy. Over the years I have fought really hard against this trait, but it seems to be an inherent characteristic.

Despite my best efforts, while I have got better at meeting new people and outwardly look more accomplished, it still feels uncomfortable on the inside. I still frequently stammer, mess up my words and look a little foolish. However, I have learnt that by moving outside my natural introverted comfort zone, taking a risk and reaching out to people to break the ice, while it does bring a risk of embarrassment, it also carries significant rewards. I persist in my discomfort and this is how I had the good fortune (we make our own luck) to meet the incredible, indefatigable Cody.

Our first meeting could from some perspectives sound very rock 'n' roll …

"She was clad head to toe in figure-hugging black Lycra. Our hearts raced. We were breathless and perspiring as our eyes met …"

Now before you jump to any conclusions, we are both happily married to other people and our meeting was not in some exotic or subversive European night club. I met Cody on a bench at the top of a hill in my local park (and before your mind wanders anywhere else, it was in broad daylight!)

We were both new members of a local running club and were supposed to be doing 'hill repeats.' These are exactly what they sound like. You run up a hill and then jog all the way down again slowly to catch your breath. This is repeated for an agreed period of time, in our case 20 minutes, or until you can't hack it any more. Great for fitness, but really hard work.

On this occasion, I had started off at way too fast a pace and was having a much-needed breather. As I sat down on the bench, Cody staggered to the summit looking like she was about to pass out. I cheekily invited her to "put your feet up and come and share a moment with me on the bench!" Thankfully my words came out okay on this occasion and she took my ice breaker the right way, put away the can of mace (okay I made that bit up) and sat on the bench with me for a rest and chat.

Our friendship developed over the coming months. Week by week I began to piece together this amazing woman's story. It is a tale of success against all the odds and a reminder that, while life can be a bumpy ride, from the low points we can soar to new heights. Now when I am having a bad day, or starting to feel sorry for myself, I have the perfect living antidote. This woman shows us how to truly laugh in the face of fear. It also illustrates the fact that if I had not had the guts to reach out to a stranger, in spite of my own shyness, I would never have had the pleasure of meeting her or learning from her.

Cody's story

Cody's own account of her life story begins in her birthplace, Zimbabwe, Africa. Back in 1987, when she was 10, while the other local children were obsessed with WWF (wrestling) and action films, Cody stood apart with her love of the television programme Carson's Law. She said she was "fascinated by the concept that you don't need a gun to make people listen. The power of the mind alone can make the world right."

Inspired by this concept, Cody felt with the passion and optimism of youth, that when she grew up, she wanted to be a lawyer. Yet the chances of this ever becoming a reality were slim. First of all, she was not an academic child. At the age of 10, she came 33rd out of 35 pupils in her class. Even more problematic was the fact that she was a girl. In 1980s Africa, female children were very much second-class citizens, deferring in almost every way to their male siblings. To compound things further, she was from a big family, so the odds of her parents being able to support her financially through law school were negligible.

In her early teens, she knuckled down and astonished everyone, including herself, by achieving 7 GCSE qualifications. Perhaps she was smarter than she had realised; maybe she was just a late starter? However, she did not have the confidence to try to persuade her parents to let her study for A-levels.

Times were hard under the Mugabe regime and putting food on the table was getting more and more difficult for her parents. Cody felt that continuing her studies would be an indulgent and unreasonable financial burden on her family. Their needs were more immediate so before her 16th birthday, she started her first job working in a departmental store, which she describes as being a bit like the British comedy "Are you being served!"

She met some interesting characters and for the first time, had her own money and was able to contribute to looking after her brothers and sisters. After a few years of pursuing different jobs and earning opportunities to ensure there was food on the family table, her childhood dream of being a lawyer began to fade further and further away.

*"Life is what happens
while you are busy making plans"*
JOHN LENNON

In the year 2000, Cody gave birth to a healthy baby boy, but her relationship with her son's father was a rocky one. Life became tough and she was forced to grow up quickly as she wrestled with the volatile relationship with her partner, the new challenge of being a mum and the continuing pressure of simply putting food on the table, now with an extra mouth to feed.

If this was not challenging enough, to compound things, the economic situation in Zimbabwe was getting desperate. Robert Mugabe's increasingly radical policies and brutal land grabs resulted in instability and economic crisis. As hyperinflation set in, the value of any money Cody did manage to earn was swiftly eroded, sometimes becoming virtually worthless before she could spend it.

Zimbabweans might have joked about being millionaires but being hungry and worrying about personal security and where the next meal was coming from, was no laughing matter. Zimbabwean billion-dollar notes entered circulation, if you were lucky you might be able to buy a loaf of bread with one. The currency quickly began to implode, as people began to refuse to exchange goods for Zimbabwean dollars at all. The black market, barter and the use of foreign currency soon became the only ways to transact. The problem for Cody and her family was that they had little to exchange, or barter with, and no access to US dollars.

Extreme times call for extreme measures and in 2004, Cody made what probably remains the most difficult single decision of her life. In desperation, she liquidated every possible resource she had access to, and bought a single airline ticket for herself to the UK. It absolutely broke her heart to leave her 4-year-old son in Zimbabwe with his paternal grandmother. However, she figured that a move to the UK would help her raise desperately needed foreign currency for her family and the opportunity of creating a better life for herself and her son if she made a success of it.

When Cody first arrived in the UK, her English was poor, which severely limited her initial job opportunities. However, hunger and the thought of the plight of her family back home gave her the drive and work ethic that astonished her employers and colleagues.

Slowly but surely, she worked her way up from the bottom rung of the career ladder. From cleaning toilets, she moved to picking and packing in a warehouse before graduating to cloakroom duties in a nightclub. Step by step, as her English and experience improved, so did her job prospects and earning power. As she began to understand British culture and society, she began to realise that whatever your background, race or colour, if you worked hard you could go places.

While working as a croupier in Manchester she met and in 2006, married an Englishman. Once again this proved to be a relatively short and rocky relationship, but like her first partner back in Africa, this marriage produced a happy legacy in the shape of a second healthy baby boy.

The breakdown of her marriage and with a toddler in tow had not stopped Cody's relentless determination to carve out a better life for herself and her burning desire to unite her 2 sons. Without the support of a partner and father figure, she was going to make this happen. Despite that absence of formal qualifications beyond her 7 GCSE's, her career continued on a relatively steady upwards trajectory, as she fulfilled increasingly technical roles, including working as a service adviser in the insurance industry and then as a data analyst.

As her earning power grew, she was able to send more money back to Africa and to afford better accommodation in the UK to ensure that the quality of life of both of her sons improved. In 2011 things really began to come together, she met Mike (now her husband) and the following year, Panashe her eldest son, was finally able to join her new family in England. Eight years after leaving Zimbabwe, she had successfully created the better life she had promised him.

With a new-found confidence in herself, enjoying the stability of a happy marriage and with her boys settled at school, for the first time in her adult life she was able to take stock and think about a more structured approach to planning her life from here on in.

After remaining dormant for over 20 years, her original Carson's Law-inspired dream of qualifying as a solicitor began to come to the fore again. An investment in a self-help book spurred her on and gave her the idea to create a vision board (wall of dreams). This took the form of a notice board upon which she and the children pinned pictures of the things they wanted to achieve. Her eldest son chose a prospectus for the sixth form college he aspired to, while her youngest pinned up a picture of the Legoland theme park, Windsor, that he wished to visit.

Inspired by the self-help book, pinning an image to the vision board meant a commitment to a dogged work ethic in the family to make each goal a reality. Knowing the magnitude of this, with butterflies in her stomach, Cody carefully pinned the prospectus for the law degree course at Manchester Metropolitan University. All 3 key objectives came to pass. Almost.

On 11 August 2014, at 6pm, Cody was scheduled to have her third and final interview for the law degree course at Manchester. It was more or less a formality before she was accepted onto the law course at Manchester University. Unfortunately, at 3pm, she also had a prior appointment of even greater potential magnitude, an appointment with a doctor. Just 3 weeks before, Cody had noticed a lump in one of her breasts. After various screening procedures, she was now due to meet with a consultant to discuss the results of a biopsy. The doctor confirmed the worst, Cody had breast cancer.

How would you react to being diagnosed with a life-threatening disease and the prospect of painful, debilitating treatment? While we all probably have an idea of how we would like to react, the truth is that there are some situations in life where you don't truly know how you will respond until it happens.

There are a number of possible scenarios. One could curl up on the couch and simply shut the world out for a while, initially unready to talk to anyone. Alternatively, one might feel the need to talk it through with our nearest and dearest, or perhaps everyone we know. We might surf the Internet to get a better understanding. Whatever the case, it is highly likely that we might cancel everything scheduled in our diaries to take time out to digest the news and begin to come to terms with things.

Cody did none of these. Just 3 hours after the diagnosis, a numb Cody was concluding her final interview at Manchester University. Somehow, she had managed to compartmentalise herself and hold it together. After little more than an hour, she had passed the interview with flying colours. Wrapping things up, the professor just had one final question. "If we offer you a place to start in September, is there anything that might interfere with your studies at the university?" Cody's response stunned the professor, who could not comprehend the bravery demonstrated, let alone the composure throughout the proceedings. Cody told her that cancer was going to be just a chapter in her book. Cancer was never going to define her, but what she was doing today, would.

Three days later a formal offer of a place arrived through Cody's letterbox. She had done it, but could she do it? Having overcome the initial shock and educated herself on the treatment ahead, Cody took the difficult, but only realistic option for her at that point. She deferred starting the course for 12 months to allow her to focus on getting better and with this 20-year goal so close to becoming a reality, she had something extra to fight for. She saw it as a mental edge.

By October 2014, with her chemotherapy well underway, as well as weariness and vomiting, the inevitable side effect of hair loss began. As you may have gleaned from my earlier depiction of my first meeting with Cody, she is an attractive woman who dresses well and takes real pride in her appearance. There was no way this woman was going to let cancer rob her of her sense of style or identity.

She decided to call her fight "lipstick and heels." This meant that she would get up every morning no matter how she felt, shower, put on her make-up and dress up like she had a first date to go to. She found that on days she did not do this, she felt worse than on the days when she made the effort. Even the hair loss from chemo was quickly turned into a positive. While the first wig she was given, in her own words made her look like "a $3 whore", Cody soon found that there were some great hairpieces available on the market and she quickly took to wearing wigs. She loved the freedom she now had that allowed her to change her hairstyle on a daily basis. She could literally change her hair to suit the occasion or outfit, definitely a female rock star trait in my book!

Yet when her eyelashes began to fall out, she found the available products much more limited. There was nothing on the market that was both comfortable to wear and looked natural and she was determined to get her normal face back.

Having had to take a leave of absence from her job to focus on her treatment, she now had time on her hands. More than this, her frequent trips to the oncology department for chemo and the fact that her life was in the balance, gave her an extra sense of urgency. As her treatment continued she began to notice the empty chairs and at the back of her mind, she equated these with people who had not made it. She felt it would have been disrespectful not to seize the day.

Although arduous, her treatment seemed to be going well, and she was determined that she was going to beat the cancer, determined to enjoy the life and the family she had strived so hard to build for herself. Determined to use the treatment time proactively, it was not enough to simply get better and get herself on the law course. She wanted to give something back and to make the experience more bearable for the patients that would follow her. Despite an extensive search, she was still unable to find a satisfactory false eyelash solution. If one did not exist, then she had decided she would create one herself.

With no prior experience of product creation, the only resources at her disposal were her gut instinct, the Internet and spare time at certain points in the chemo cycle when she felt well enough to concentrate. Step by step, she educated herself. After countless hours of online research and hundreds of dead ends, she finally managed to narrow down her search to a handful of UK companies that specialised in creating prototypes. After speaking to each of them on the phone, she used her gut instinct to seek out the one she felt most comfortable with. She then invested a high percentage of her own modest savings in turning the concept into reality.

This was not an easy process, her chosen prototyper was based in Essex some 200 miles away. After numerous iterations, she finally had the prototype samples of false eyelashes that did exactly what she wanted. They looked great and they were comfortable to wear and unlike all the other products designed for the mainstream market, they did not need to be fixed onto existing eyelashes.

Furthermore, on 9 April 2015, Cody received the all clear. The combination of chemotherapy and her determination had successfully seen off the cancer.

Cody had come a long way, but the mission was still far from complete. As anyone that watches Dragons' Den will know, having and developing a new idea, or product, is only half the battle. Taking a prototype to market and mass producing it in a way that makes money, is truly the hard part, but this woman was not going to be deterred.

Having explored numerous avenues without success for a good half year following the all clear, the initial breakthrough came via a local business competition where she pitched her idea and won. She then took things to the next level by pitching her idea at a national competition at the Business Show in London, where astonishingly, her pitch won again.

As well as some fantastic local and national exposure, the prize for both competitions was business mentoring services. Very quickly she had well-connected professional business consultants giving her advice and opening the right doors to ensure that her powerful story of triumph and inspiration in the face of adversity was getting her brilliant prototype C-lashes in front of the right people.

By the spring of 2016, she had secured firm interest from the UK's leading pharmacy chain to stock the product that in turn put her in touch with a partner company to help her mass produce and brand the product. I think it is safe to say that Cody is about to become a Rock Star businesswoman.

There is still the small matter of that law degree to be taken care of. It remains firmly pinned to Cody's vision board. However, she quite rightly has deferred it for another few years to allow her to focus on the launch of the C-lash range of products and the PR work she will need to do to support it.

So what lessons can we take from this story?

1. If I had stayed within my shell and had not overcome my natural shyness, then I might never have had the pleasure of meeting Cody.

2. The more I look, the more amazing people I find. The world is surprisingly full of exceptional people, we just have to actively seek them out. I am convinced that by spending time in the company of great people, we can be inspired to be better ourselves. I find optimism and enthusiasm infectious, it makes me dare to dream.

3. I believe that we all have the ability to do amazing things. Unfortunately though, too often it takes adversity to bring out this greatness. I have made it my life's work to try to find out how to help people achieve more without the need for a negative catalyst.

4. For most of us, life and success does not come easily. Cody dealt with setback after setback before she triumphed.

5. Be flexible. If something even better than your original goal comes along, don't be afraid to upgrade.

Lesson 10 Exercise

So, assuming that you are not a real-life rock star, but that you do manage to dodge that bus and remain in good health for many years to come and having reflected on your current legacy (you may want to re-read your answers to the previous exercise), what would you like your future legacy to be? What elements are you going to change? **This exercise is important. You genuinely can write your own legacy, so let's write it down!**

_____

_____

_____

_____

Creating a Rock Star Legacy

Why Belief and Meaning Are Key to a Successful and Happy Retirement

Creating your own unique plan and vision, feeling that you are shaping your own life, 'writing your own story', is highly empowering.

No matter how committed you are to taking control, the journey is never a linear process of continuous wins. Life will throw things up that get in the way and there will be setbacks.

Selectively take the good omens and ignore the bad ones to help you along the way.

In an increasingly busy world with a million things competing for our time and attention, it is important to proactively build in blocks of quality time, away from the normal hubbub and distractions, to take stock, review and update our plans to make sure we stay on track

Being mindful of the long-term consequences of the life-journey we are on, at as early a point as possible, is likely to lead to greater fulfilment and satisfaction. Life is littered with "successful" rock stars and superficially "successful" people who fulfilled their solely self-serving dreams and found them to be ultimately hollow, unfulfilling and lonely.

The old adage that giving, rather than receiving gifts, brings far greater pleasure, is true.

Ensuring that our life plans build in sufficient thought to our legacy ensures a much greater chance of long-term happiness and satisfaction. I see this almost every day in my work as a business consultant. Having a genuine purpose beyond our own desires greatly increases our chance of success. For example, if you are a business owner and genuinely care for the welfare of your staff, customers and even your suppliers, then your business is much more likely to succeed and create wealth in the long term than a ruthlessly hard-nosed business person seeking to extract maximum short-term profit.

Maintaining an optimistic outlook and helping people in genuine need by going that extra mile and doing so without expectation of reward or reciprocity, often leads to very happy unexpected consequences. Sometimes people may take advantage of "givers", but the odd low is worth the soaring high points and experiences that will form part of your legacy and life journey, more than making up for this.

Money may be part of it, but it is probably the least important metric against which to consider and measure your legacy. The input of your time, experience and unique qualities via acts of love, kindness, nurturing and mentoring of people not just within your family, but your wider sphere of influence, are the things that will have the biggest impact and provide the greatest sense of satisfaction, pride and legacy.

CONCLUSION

"There is an awful lot of unfulfilled potential to be found in the graveyard" [86]

KADIWA M GAPARE

I believe that the seeds of greatness lie within all men. Many of us show brief flashes of the light inside, but for the most part, our remarkable potential remains dormant, waiting for a spark that, if left to chance, may come too late. Nature provides some wonderful natural parallels. To thrive long-term in the wild, certain plant species need dramatic, seemingly brutal external environmental factors to intervene. Forest fires cause massive immediate destruction, yet they are essential for the renewal and long-term health of many woodland ecosystems. Fruit trees

---

[86] in spite of the media's obsession with the negative.

require extreme winter conditions and a severe frost to stimulate them to produce an optimal harvest in the autumn season that follows. Counter-intuitively, milder, seemingly more clement winter conditions actually lead to poor harvests.

It seems to me that humans follow the same pattern. For most of us it takes adverse conditions, a winter of discontent in our lives to bring out the best in us, to help us truly bear fruit and live the life we are capable of. Too frequently, a health scare, or the loss of a parent, sibling or partner are needed to remind us of our own mortality and the fact that the clock is ticking, to ignite the passions within us to **be** more, to **see** more and to **do** more. Many of the case studies and stories cited in this book, from my boyhood idol Douglas Bader, to my newly discovered heroine, Codilla Gapore illustrate exactly this: greatness in the face of adversity. These incredible people show us how we can turn what life throws at us to our advantage, to face challenges and to use them to motivate us to reshape our lives to greater things.

ROCK STAR EXAMPLE

Eric Clapton's ballad "Tears in Heaven" was written in 1991 by the broken-hearted Clapton after his 4-year-old son's tragic death. It is deemed by critics and fans alike to be his most emotive composition and recording performance.

Yet although being able to turn adversity into victory is an admirable quality, it is clearly not a great life plan to wait passively for lightning to strike. Surely there has to be a better way than to rely on pain, fear, loss or adversity to stimulate a new action plan, to alter your current path?

As I have been at pains to convey throughout this book, for those of us lucky enough to be born in the 21st century,[87] we truly have never had it so good. Perhaps it is the success of our highly advanced capitalist industrial society and the resulting lack of genuine physical hunger that is to blame for our lack of hunger in a higher sense? Maybe it is the overwhelming abundance, the number of life choices and available information competing for our attention that clouds our vision and dilutes our focus? So, the big question for me is "do we really need to walk in the dark, to reach the light?" Do we need a short, sharp shock to wake us up from our complacency, to achieve the life we want? To wake ourselves from slumber and earn a Rock Star Retirement of our own design?

Looking back through the numerous stories and case studies, while all are admirable, the ones that stand out as being the most aspirational are perhaps, somewhat surprisingly, the least dramatic ones. The examples where the protagonists took action of their own accord. The ones with no dramas.

Remember my friend Ian from chapter one? He moved from Manchester to New Zealand without a single specific negative stimulus. He simply mapped out and elected to follow a different life plan, allowing him to live the life he wanted from a very young age.

Remember too, Bruce and Sheila Napier living their dream life on a canal barge? To me this is a truly commendable example of a couple who proactively achieved their Rock Star Retirement without the need for a direct negative external influence. They forwent normal life planning and beat the system. While they might not see themselves this way, to me they are the ultimate Rock Star Retirees. Although they still have many years to go before they get there, you will not find Ian or the Napiers staring aimlessly out of their windows in their final years wishing and wondering what might have been. And having read this book, I hope that neither will you. Whatever your dreams and ambitions, I wish you every success in achieving them. Remember it is never too

---

[87] in spite of the media's obsession with the negative

late to seize the day — and what a day and a life it could be, if you truly put your mind to it.

On Tour ...

So that's it...you now have the knowledge and framework to create YOUR Rock Star Retirement and to live life your way.

Of course learning to Rock takes practice. If you would like further tuition and help in cranking your internal amplifier up to 11, then we invite you to sign-up to our website; www.rockstarretirement.com. Here you will find additional practical resources, case studies and video content to help you with your journey.

We would also love your feedback on this book, please do leave a review on Amazon. It would also be great to hear how you are getting on with your Rock Star Retirement.